ANTITRUST GUIDELINES FOR INTERNATIONAL ENFORCEMENT AND COOPERATION

Issued by the:

U.S. DEPARTMENT OF JUSTICE

and

FEDERAL TRADE COMMISSION

January 13, 2017

TABLE OF CONTENTS

1. Introduction 1

2. Relevant Antitrust and Related Statutes 4

   2.1 Sherman Antitrust Act 4

   2.2 Federal Trade Commission Act 5

   2.3 Clayton Antitrust Act 6

   2.4 Hart-Scott-Rodino Antitrust Improvements Act of 1976 7

   2.5 Antitrust Criminal Penalty Enhancement
       and Reform Act of 2004 9

   2.6 International Antitrust Enforcement Assistance Act 10

   2.7 National Cooperative Research and Production Act 11

   2.8 Webb-Pomerene Act 12

   2.9 Export Trading Company Act of 1982 12

   2.10 Wilson Tariff Act 15

   2.11 Trade Act of 1974, Section 301 15

   2.12 Tariff Act of 1930 15

3. Agencies' Application of U.S. Antitrust Law to Conduct Involving
Foreign Commerce 16

   3.1 Conduct Involving Import Commerce 19

   3.2 Conduct Involving Non-Import Foreign Commerce 21

   3.3 Conduct Involving U.S. Government Financing or Purchasing 26

4. Agencies' Consideration of Foreign Jurisdictions 27

   4.1 Comity 27

4.2 Consideration of Foreign Government Involvement **29**

4.2.1 Foreign Sovereign Immunity *30*

4.2.2 Foreign Sovereign Compulsion *32*

4.2.3 Act of State Doctrine *35*

4.2.4 Petitioning of Sovereigns *36*

5. International Cooperation **37**

5.1 Investigations and Cooperation **38**

5.1.1 Investigative Tools *38*

5.1.2 Confidentiality *40*

5.1.3 Legal Bases for Cooperation *42*

5.1.4 Types of Information Exchanged and Waivers of Confidentiality *44*

5.1.5 Remedies *47*

5.2 Special Considerations in Criminal Investigations **49**

Annex 1. Defined Terms **A1**

1. Introduction

"The heart of our national economic policy long has been faith in the value of competition,"[1] and the U.S. antitrust laws have stood as the ultimate protector of competition in our free market economy. That policy and these laws rest "on the premise that the unrestrained interaction of competitive forces will yield the best allocation of our economic resources, the lowest prices, the highest quality and the greatest material progress."[2] To protect U.S. consumers and businesses from anticompetitive conduct in foreign commerce, the federal antitrust laws have applied to "commerce with foreign nations" since their inception.[3]

Since the 1995 release of the Antitrust Enforcement Guidelines for International Operations, trade between the United States and other countries has expanded at a tremendous rate. With this expansion, the federal antitrust laws have played an increasingly important role in protecting consumers and businesses purchasing in U.S. import commerce and exporters selling in U.S. export commerce from anticompetitive conduct. In addition, anticompetitive conduct—from price-fixing cartels to competition-reducing mergers and monopolization—increasingly is subject to investigation and, in some cases, remedial action by foreign authorities.

The Department of Justice (the "Department") and the Federal Trade Commission (the "Commission" or "FTC") (collectively the "Agencies") are charged with enforcement of the federal antitrust laws, an essential component of which is the application of these laws to foreign commerce. Moreover, the Agencies cooperate on their antitrust enforcement with foreign authorities wherever appropriate.

In furtherance of that enforcement and in recognition of the role of international cooperation, the Agencies issue these Antitrust Guidelines for International Enforcement and Cooperation ("International Guidelines"), which replace the 1995 Antitrust Enforcement Guidelines for International Operations. The International Guidelines provide updated guidance to businesses engaged in international activities on questions that concern the Agencies' international enforcement policy as well as the Agencies' related investigative tools and cooperation with foreign authorities.

---

[1] *Standard Oil Co. v. Fed. Trade Comm'n*, 340 U.S. 231, 248 (1951).

[2] *N. Pac. Ry. Co. v. United States*, 356 U.S. 1, 4 (1958).

[3] *See infra* Sections 3.1 and 3.2 for a discussion of the meaning of "commerce with foreign nations."

Many nations share our faith in the value of competition, and as of 2017, over 130 jurisdictions have enacted antitrust laws as a means to ensure open and free markets, promote consumer welfare, and prevent conduct that impedes competition. Accordingly, the Agencies have expanded their efforts and committed greater resources to building and maintaining strong relationships with foreign authorities to promote greater policy engagement. This engagement with foreign authorities has multiple goals, notably: increasing global understanding of different jurisdictions' respective antitrust laws, policies, and procedures; contributing to procedural and substantive convergence toward best practices; and facilitating enforcement cooperation internationally. The Agencies have championed and continue to promote this engagement, focusing on substantive enforcement standards that seek to advance consumer welfare based on sound economics, procedural fairness, transparency, and non-discriminatory treatment of parties.

In furtherance of these goals, the Agencies raise important policy and practical antitrust issues with foreign authorities bilaterally and through multilateral organizations such as the Competition Committee of the Organisation for Economic Co-operation and Development ("OECD"), the International Competition Network ("ICN"), the United Nations Conference on Trade and Development ("UNCTAD"), and the Asia-Pacific Economic Cooperation ("APEC") forum. These efforts have resulted in the development and implementation of standards of international best practice and consensus guidance on substantive antitrust and procedural fairness.[4] Consistent approaches to competition law, policy, and procedures across jurisdictions facilitate cooperation among competition agencies, and increase the effectiveness and predictability of enforcement, which benefits the Agencies, consumers, and the business community.

In the United States, the Agencies are responsible for international antitrust policy engagement and cooperation. The Agencies also work within the U.S. government to

---

[4] *See, e.g.,* Int'l Competition Network, *Guidance on Investigative Process,* http://www.internationalcompetitionnetwork.org/uploads/library/doc1028.pdf; Org. for Econ. Co-Operation & Dev., *Recommendation Concerning International Co-operation on Competition Investigations and Proceedings* (2014), http://www.oecd.org/daf/competition/2014-rec-internat-coop-competition.pdf; Int'l Competition Network, *Recommended Practices on the Assessment of Dominance/Substantial Market Power;* http://www.internationalcompetitionnetwork.org/uploads/library/doc317.pdf; Int'l Competition Network, *Recommended Practices for Merger Notification and Review Procedures,* http://www.internationalcompetitionnetwork.org/uploads/library/doc588.pdf; Org. for Econ. Co-Operation & Dev., *Recommendation Concerning Effective Action Against Hard Core Cartels* (1998), https://www.oecd.org/daf/competition/2350130.pdf.

ensure that broader U.S. policy and engagement appropriately reflects an understanding of complex international antitrust issues and accepted principles of competition law, economics, and policy. Consumers and businesses are welcome to contact the Agencies concerning the application and enforcement of antitrust law and policy internationally.

In addition to this introductory chapter, the International Guidelines are divided into four other chapters. Chapter 2 provides a brief summary of the antitrust and related laws that are likely to have the greatest significance for businesses engaged in international activities. Chapter 3 describes what connections to the United States are sufficient for the Agencies to investigate or bring enforcement actions challenging conduct occurring abroad or involving or affecting foreign commerce. Chapter 4 describes the Agencies' consideration of international comity concerns and the role of foreign government involvement in determining whether to open an investigation or bring an enforcement action. Chapter 5 provides guidance on the Agencies' pertinent investigatory tools and their enforcement cooperation with foreign authorities. These International Guidelines also include a number of examples that are intended to illustrate how the principles and policies discussed may operate in certain contexts.[5]

As is the case with all guidelines issued by the Agencies, users should rely on qualified counsel to assist them in evaluating the antitrust risk associated with any contemplated transaction or activity.[6] No set of guidelines could possibly indicate how the Agencies will assess the particular facts of every case. Persons seeking more specific advance statements of enforcement intentions with respect to the issues discussed in the International Guidelines should use other procedures, which may include the Department's Business Review procedure[7] and the Commission's Advisory Opinion procedure.[8] Other existing Department and Commission guidelines and statements are not qualified, modified, or otherwise amended by the

---

[5] The ultimate outcome of the analysis in a particular case, *i.e.,* in determining whether or not a violation of the federal antitrust laws has occurred, or the manner in which the Agencies may cooperate with foreign authorities, depends on the specific facts and circumstances of the case.

[6] Users also should evaluate separately the risk of private litigation by competitors, consumers, and suppliers, as well as the risk of enforcement by state prosecutors under state and federal antitrust laws.

[7] 28 C.F.R. § 50.6.

[8] 16 C.F.R. §§ 1.1-1.4.

issuance of these International Guidelines. The International Guidelines are not intended to, do not, and may not be relied upon to create any rights, substantive or procedural, enforceable at law by any party in any matter, civil or criminal. Nor are any limitations hereby placed on otherwise lawful litigative prerogatives of the Department or Commission.

2. Relevant Antitrust and Related Statutes

Cases involving foreign commerce or foreign conduct can involve almost any provision of the federal antitrust laws. The Agencies do not discriminate in the enforcement of the antitrust laws based on the nationality of the parties. Nor do the Agencies employ their statutory authority to further non-antitrust goals. When the Agencies determine that a sufficient nexus to the United States exists to apply the antitrust laws[9] and that neither international comity nor the involvement of a foreign jurisdiction precludes investigation or enforcement,[10] the Agencies apply the same substantive rules to all cases. The following is a brief summary of the antitrust and related statutes that are likely to have the greatest significance for businesses engaged in international activities.

2.1 Sherman Antitrust Act

The Sherman Antitrust Act ("Sherman Act") sets forth general antitrust prohibitions.[11] Section 1 of the Sherman Act outlaws contracts, combinations, and conspiracies that unreasonably restrain "trade or commerce among the several States, or with foreign nations."[12] Section 2 outlaws monopolization, attempts to monopolize, and conspiracies to monopolize "any part of the trade or commerce among the several States, or with foreign nations."[13] Section 6a, added by the Foreign Trade Antitrust Improvements Act of 1982 ("FTAIA"), clarifies the Sherman Act's application to conduct involving only non-import foreign commerce.[14]

---

[9] *See infra* Sections 3.1-3.3.

[10] *See infra* Sections 4.1-4.2.

[11] 15 U.S.C. §§ 1-7.

[12] *Id.* § 1.

[13] *Id.* § 2.

[14] *Id.* § 6a; *see infra* Sections 2.9, 3.1, and 3.2.

Violations of the Sherman Act may be prosecuted as civil or criminal offenses. The Department has sole responsibility for the criminal enforcement of the Sherman Act and criminally prosecutes traditional per se offenses of the law, which typically involve price fixing, customer allocation, bid rigging, or other cartel activities that would also be violations of the law in many countries. Criminal violations of the Act are punishable by fines and imprisonment. The Sherman Act provides that corporate defendants may be fined up to $100 million and individual defendants may be fined up to $1 million and sentenced to up to 10 years imprisonment.[15]

In a civil proceeding, the Department may obtain equitable relief to prevent and restrain violations of the Sherman Act.[16] It may also obtain treble damages if the U.S. government is injured in its business or property by a violation, for example as a purchaser of affected goods or services.[17] Private plaintiffs may also obtain injunctive and treble damage relief for violations of the Sherman Act.[18]

2.2 Federal Trade Commission Act

Section 5 of the Federal Trade Commission Act ("FTC Act") declares unlawful "unfair methods of competition in or affecting commerce, and unfair or deceptive acts or practices in or affecting commerce."[19] Pursuant to its authority to prevent unfair methods of competition, the Commission may take administrative action against conduct that violates the Sherman Act or the Clayton Antitrust Act ("Clayton Act"), as well as anticompetitive practices that do not fall within the scope

---

[15] 15 U.S.C. §§ 1-3. Defendants may be fined up to twice the gross pecuniary gain or loss caused by their offense in lieu of the Sherman Act fines, pursuant to 18 U.S.C. § 3571(d). Defendants may also be placed on probation for up to five years. The U.S. Sentencing Commission Guidelines provide advisory sentences or sentencing ranges for antitrust offenses. *See* U.S.S.G. § 2R1.1 & ch. 8. In determining the appropriate sentence, the court must consider the Guidelines' advisory sentence or sentencing range, as well as the other factors in 18 U.S.C. § 3553(a) and also, for fines, the factors in 18 U.S.C. § 3572(a). The Department generally seeks sentences consistent with the Guidelines.

[16] 15 U.S.C. § 4.

[17] *Id.* § 15a.

[18] *See id.* §§ 15, 26.

[19] *Id.* § 45.

of the Sherman or Clayton Acts.[20] The Commission may also seek injunctive relief in federal court under Section 13(b) of the FTC Act.[21] These International Guidelines pertain only to the Commission's antitrust enforcement authority under Section 5's prohibition of unfair methods of competition. Section 5(a)(3) of the FTC Act, added by the Foreign Trade Antitrust Improvements Act of 1982, clarifies the FTC Act's application to conduct involving only non-import foreign commerce.[22]

2.3 Clayton Antitrust Act

The Clayton Act expands on the general prohibitions of the Sherman Act and addresses anticompetitive problems in their incipiency.[23] Section 7 of the Clayton Act prohibits any merger or acquisition of stock or assets "where in any line of commerce or in any activity affecting commerce in any section of the country, the effect of such acquisition may be substantially to lessen competition, or to tend to create a monopoly."[24] The Agency reviewing a transaction that would violate Section 7 can seek a federal court order enjoining its consummation.[25] In addition,

---

[20] *Id.* § 45(b). *See* Fed. Trade Comm'n, *Statement of Enforcement Principles Regarding "Unfair methods of Competition" Under Section 5 of the FTC Act*, https://www.ftc.gov/public-statements/2015/08/statement-enforcement-principles-regarding-unfair-methods-competition.

[21] 15 U.S.C. § 53(b).

[22] *Id.* § 45(a)(3).

[23] *Id.* §§ 12-27. Under the Clayton Act, "commerce" includes "trade or commerce among the several States and with foreign nations," and "person" includes corporations or associations existing under or authorized either by the laws of the United States or any of its states or territories, or by the laws of any foreign country. *Id.* § 12.

[24] *Id.* § 18. The asset acquisition clause applies to "person[s] subject to the jurisdiction of the Federal Trade Commission" under the Clayton Act.

[25] *Id.* § 25 (Clayton Act); *id.* § 53(b) (FTC Act). On August 19, 2010, the Agencies issued revised Horizontal Merger Guidelines, which outline their principal analytical techniques, practices, and enforcement policy with respect to mergers and acquisitions involving actual or potential competitors under the federal antitrust laws. U.S. Dep't of Justice & Fed. Trade Comm'n, *Horizontal Merger Guidelines* (2010), https://www.justice.gov/sites/default/files/atr/legacy/2010/08/19/hmg-2010.pdf.

the Commission may seek a cease and desist order in an administrative proceeding against a merger under Section 11 of the Clayton Act, Section 5 of the FTC Act, or both.[26] Private parties and state Attorneys General may also seek injunctive relief under the Clayton Act.[27]

Section 3 of the Clayton Act prohibits any person engaged in commerce from conditioning the lease or sale of goods or commodities upon the purchaser's agreement not to use the products of a competitor, if the effect may be "to substantially lessen competition or tend to create a monopoly in any line of commerce."[28] In evaluating transactions, courts use the same analysis employed in the evaluation of tying under Section 1 of the Sherman Act to assess a defendant's liability under Section 3 of the Clayton Act.[29]

Section 2 of the Clayton Act, as amended by the Robinson-Patman Act,[30] prohibits price discrimination in certain circumstances. In practice, the Commission has exercised principal responsibility for enforcing this provision.

2.4 Hart-Scott-Rodino Antitrust Improvements Act of 1976

Title II of the Hart-Scott-Rodino Antitrust Improvements Act of 1976 ("HSR Act") facilitates the Agencies' enforcement of the antitrust laws with respect to anticompetitive mergers and acquisitions. It requires that persons provide notice to the Agencies of certain proposed mergers or acquisitions and imposes a waiting

---

[26] 15 U.S.C. § 21 (Clayton Act); *id.* § 45 (FTC Act).

[27] *Id.* §§ 15c, 26.

[28] *Id.* § 14.

[29] *See, e.g.*, *Sheridan v. Marathon Petroleum Co.*, 530 F.3d 590, 592 (7th Cir. 2008) ("Though some old cases say otherwise, the standards for adjudicating tying under the two statutes are now recognized to be the same.").

[30] 15 U.S.C. §§ 13-13b, 21a. The Robinson-Patman Act applies only to purchases involving commodities "for use, consumption, or resale within the United States." *Id.* § 13(a). It has been construed not to apply to sales for export. *See, e.g.*, *Gen. Chem., Inc. v. Exxon Chem. Co.*, 625 F.2d 1231, 1234 (5th Cir. 1980). Intervening domestic sales, however, would be subject to the Act. *See Raul Int'l Corp. v. Sealed Power Corp.*, 586 F. Supp. 349, 351-55 (D.N.J. 1984).

period on these mergers or acquisitions.[31] Transactions are subject to these requirements only if they meet certain conditions, including minimum size thresholds.[32] Some transactions are explicitly exempted from these requirements by the statute's text.[33] The HSR Act and the Hart-Scott-Rodino Premerger Notification Rules ("HSR Rules")[34] exempt from the notification requirements certain international transactions (typically those having little nexus to U.S. commerce) that otherwise meet the statutory thresholds.[35] Transactions not subject to the HSR Act's notification and waiting period requirements may still be subject to the Sherman Act, the FTC Act, or the Clayton Act, and the Agencies may seek to block or undo an anticompetitive merger or acquisition or seek other equitable relief when any of those statutes applies.

If a transaction is subject to the HSR Act's requirements, the parties must typically wait 30 days after providing notice to the Agencies before they may consummate it; the parties to cash tender offers must wait only 15 days.[36] The Agency reviewing the transaction may request additional documents or information concerning a transaction, known as a "Second Request," during this waiting period. Issuing a Second Request extends the waiting period until a certain number of days after the

---

[31] 15 U.S.C. § 18a. The scope of the Agencies' jurisdiction under Section 7 of the Clayton Act, *id.* § 18, exceeds the scope of those transactions subject to the premerger notification requirements of the HSR Act. Enforcement responsibility in particular cases is allocated to either the Department or the Commission typically based on prior agency expertise in the relevant product market at issue.

[32] *Id.* § 18a(a). As a result of a 2000 amendment to the HSR Act, all minimum thresholds in the Act are adjusted annually based on changes in the gross national product. *Id.* § 18a(a)(2). The adjusted annual thresholds are announced in January of each year in the Federal Register, and are effective 30 days after publication. The current adjusted annual thresholds are available on the Commission's website at https://www.ftc.gov/enforcement/premerger-notification-program/current-thresholds.

[33] 15 U.S.C.§ 18a(c).

[34] 16 C.F.R. pt. 801-03.

[35] 16 C.F.R. §§ 801.1(e), (k) & 802.50-53.

[36] 15 U.S.C. § 18a(b); 16 C.F.R. § 803.1; *see also* 11 U.S.C. § 363 (b)(2) (regarding certain transactions involving parties in bankruptcy).

Agency has received the requested material and the party certifies substantial compliance; typically 30 days, but only 10 days for cash tender offers.[37]

Failure to comply with the HSR Act is punishable by court-imposed and potentially substantial civil monetary penalties.[38] A court also may order injunctive relief to remedy a substantial failure to comply with the HSR Act.[39]

The HSR Act and the HSR Rules are necessarily technical and should be consulted directly. Businesses may seek an interpretation of their obligations under the HSR Act and the HSR Rules from the Commission's Premerger Notification Office.[40]

2.5 Antitrust Criminal Penalty Enhancement and Reform Act of 2004

The Antitrust Criminal Penalty Enhancement and Reform Act of 2004 ("ACPERA") limits the liability for civil damages claims in private state or federal antitrust actions of a qualifying person cooperating with a criminal antitrust investigation by the Department.[41] Specifically, for claims against a corporation that enters into an antitrust leniency agreement with the Department pursuant to its Corporate Leniency Policy[42] or a cooperating individual covered by such an agreement, a claimant cannot recover damages exceeding the "portion of the actual damages sustained by such claimant which is attributable to the commerce done by the applicant in the goods or services affected by the violation."[43] To qualify for this

---

[37] 15 U.S.C. § 18a(e).

[38] *Id.* § 18a(g)(1). In August 2016, the limit on these penalties was adjusted upward to $40,000 for each day a violation continues. That limit adjusts periodically based on inflation. 28 U.S.C. § 2461 note; 16 C.F.R. § 1.98(a).

[39] 15 U.S.C. § 18a(g)(2).

[40] *See* 16 C.F.R. § 803.30.

[41] Pub. L. 108-237, 118 Stat. 661 (codified as 15 U.S.C. § 1 note). Originally set to expire in 2009, the provision has been twice extended. Pub. L. 111-190, 124 Stat. 1275 (2010); Pub. L. 111-30, 123 Stat. 1775 (2009). It is currently set to expire, absent further extension by Congress, on June 22, 2020.

[42] For information on the Department's Antitrust Corporate Leniency Policy, see https://www.justice.gov/atr/leniency-program.

[43] 15 U.S.C. § 1 note.

limitation, the corporation or cooperating individuals must meet the conditions of the Corporate Leniency Policy, including cooperating fully with the Department's investigation, and must meet certain requirements in connection with the claimant's civil action. These requirements include providing the claimant with a full account of all facts known to the corporation or cooperating individual that are potentially relevant to the civil action, furnishing the claimant with potentially relevant documents and other items wherever located, and, in the case of cooperating individuals, making himself or herself available for interviews, depositions, or testimony in connection with the civil action as the claimant may reasonably require.

2.6 International Antitrust Enforcement Assistance Act

The International Antitrust Enforcement Assistance Act ("IAEAA")[44] authorizes the Agencies to enter into antitrust-specific mutual assistance agreements with foreign authorities.[45] Under such agreements, U.S. and foreign authorities may share evidence relating to antitrust violations already in their possession and provide each other with investigatory assistance in obtaining evidence, including statutorily protected confidential information.[46] The IAEAA does not apply to materials submitted pursuant to the HSR Act.[47] The Agencies entered into an IAEAA agreement with Australia in 1999.[48]

---

[44] 15 U.S.C. § 6201 *et seq.*

[45] Information relevant to antitrust enforcement may also be provided under generalized legal assistance treaties in force between the United States and a wide range of foreign partners. *See infra* Sections 5.1.3 and 5.2.

[46] 15 U.S.C. § 6201. Agreements entered into under the IAEAA's authority must include, among other requirements, assurances that the foreign authority will protect the confidentiality of the information exchanged, *id.* § 6211(2)(A)-(C), and provisions addressing the permitted use of the evidence exchanged, *id.* § 6211(2)(E)(i), (ii).

[47] *Id.* § 6204(1).

[48] Agreement Between the Government of the United States of America and The Government of Australia on Mutual Antitrust Enforcement Assistance, U.S.-Aus. (1999), *reprinted in* 4 Trade Rep. Reg. (CCH) ¶ 13,502A, *available at* https://www.ftc.gov/policy/cooperation-agreements/usaaustralia-mutual-antitrust-enforcement-assistance-agreement.

2.7 National Cooperative Research and Production Act

The National Cooperative Research and Production Act ("NCRPA"), as amended by the Standards Development Organization Advancement Act of 2004,[49] clarifies the substantive application of the state and federal antitrust laws to joint ventures and standards development organizations ("SDOs") while engaged in standards development activity. It requires U.S. courts to judge the competitive effects of a challenged joint venture or SDO covered by the Act under a rule-of-reason standard.[50] This approach is consistent with the Agencies' general analysis of joint ventures.[51] The Act further provides for the possible recovery of attorney's fees by joint ventures and SDOs that are prevailing parties in damage actions brought against them under the antitrust laws.

The NCRPA also establishes a voluntary procedure pursuant to which parties to a joint venture or an SDO that meet certain criteria may notify the Agencies of their intention to engage in standards development activity. Under the statute, if participants provide notice to the Agencies, the amount of monetary relief obtainable in a private civil suit challenging the standards-development activity is limited to actual, rather than treble, damages so long as the challenged conduct is within the scope of the notification. This benefit is not available to joint production ventures, unless "(1) the principal facilities for such production are located in the

---

[49] 15 U.S.C. §§ 4301-06.

[50] *Id.* § 4302.

[51] *See, e.g.*, U.S. Dep't of Justice & Fed. Trade Comm'n, *Antitrust Guidelines for the Licensing of Intellectual Property* 5 (2017), https://www.justice.gov/atr/IPguidelines/download; Fed. Trade Comm'n & U.S. Dep't of Justice, *Antitrust Guidelines for Collaborations Among Competitors*, (2000), *available at* https://www.ftc.gov/sites/default/files/documents/public_events/ joint-venture-hearings-antitrust-guidelines-collaboration-among-competitors/ ftcdojguidelines-2.pdf; Fed. Trade Comm'n & U.S. Dep't of Justice, *Statements of Antitrust Enforcement Policy in Health Care*, Stmt. 2 (1996), *available at* https://www.ftc.gov/sites/default/files/attachments/competition-policy-guidance/ statements_of_antitrust_enforcement_policy_in_health_care_august_1996.pdf (outlining a four-step approach for joint venture analysis). *See generally Am. Needle, Inc. v. Nat'l Football League*, 560 U.S. 183 (2010); *Texaco, Inc. v. Dagher*, 547 U.S. 1 (2006); *Fed. Trade Comm'n v. Ind. Fed'n of Dentists*, 476 U.S. 447 (1986); *Nat'l Collegiate Athletic Ass'n v. Bd. of Regents of Univ. of Okla.*, 468 U.S. 85 (1984). *See generally also In re Mass. Board of Registration in Optometry*, 110 F.T.C. 549 (1988).

United States or its territories, and (2) each person who controls any party to such venture (including such party itself) is a United States person, or a foreign person from a country whose law accords antitrust treatment no less favorable to United States persons than to such country's domestic persons with respect to participation in joint ventures for production."[52]

2.8 Webb-Pomerene Act

The Webb-Pomerene Act provides a limited antitrust exemption for the formation and operation of associations of otherwise competing businesses to engage collectively in export sales.[53] The exemption applies only to the export of "goods, wares, or merchandise."[54] It does not apply to conduct that has an anticompetitive effect in the United States or that injures domestic competitors of the members of an export association. Nor does it provide any immunity from prosecution under foreign antitrust laws.[55] Associations seeking an exemption under the Webb-Pomerene Act must file their articles of agreement and annual reports with the Commission, but pre-formation approval from the Commission is not required. Few associations file reports with the FTC; those reports are available on the Commission's website.[56]

2.9 Export Trading Company Act of 1982

The Export Trading Company Act of 1982 ("ETC Act")[57] is designed to increase U.S. exports of goods and services in several ways.[58] In Title II, it encourages more

---

[52] 15 U.S.C. § 4306(2).

[53] *Id.* §§ 61-65.

[54]*Id.* § 61.

[55] *See, e.g.*, Case C-89/85, *Ahlström v. Comm'n*, 1988 E.C.R. 5193 (finding Webb-Pomerene association was not exempt from violations of European antitrust law); Commission Decision of 19 December 1990 Relating to a Proceeding Under Article 85 of the EEC Treaty, 1991 O.J. (L 152) 16-20 (denying antitrust exemption to soda ash Webb-Pomerene association); *Competition Comm'n v. Am. Nat. Soda Ash Corp.*, 2008 ZACT 92 (South Africa) (settlement by Webb-Pomerene association with Competition Tribunal South Africa for violations of antitrust laws).

[56] Webb-Pomerene Act filings are available at https://www.ftc.gov/policy/reports/webb-pomerene-act-filings. Two associations filed reports with the FTC for 2015.

[57] Pub L. No. 97-290, 96 Stat. 1233 (codified in scattered sections of 15 U.S.C.).

efficient provision of export trade services to U.S. producers and suppliers by reducing restrictions on trade financing provided by financial institutions.[59] In Title III, it reduces uncertainty concerning the application of the U.S. antitrust laws to export trade through the creation of a procedure by which persons engaging in U.S. export trade may obtain an export trade certificate of review ("ETCR").[60] In Title IV, also known as the Foreign Trade Antitrust Improvement Act of 1982 or FTAIA, it clarifies the application of the Sherman Act and the FTC Act to conduct involving only non-import foreign commerce.[61] The Title III certificates are discussed briefly here; the application of the Sherman Act and FTC Act is treated below in Chapter 3.

Export trade certificates of review are issued by the Secretary of Commerce with the concurrence of the Department. Persons named in the ETCR obtain limited immunity from suit under both federal and state antitrust laws for activities that are specified in the certificate and that comply with the terms of the certificate.[62] To obtain an ETCR, an applicant must show that proposed export conduct will:

1. result in neither a substantial lessening of competition or restraint of trade within the United States nor a substantial restraint of the export trade of any competitor of the applicant;
2. not unreasonably enhance, stabilize, or depress prices in the United States of the class of goods or services covered by the application;
3. not constitute unfair methods of competition against competitors engaged in the export of the class of goods or services exported by the applicant; and
4. not include any act that may reasonably be expected to result in the sale for consumption or resale in the United States of such goods or services.[63]

Congress intended that these standards "encompass the full range of the antitrust laws," as defined in the ETC Act.[64]

---

[58] 15 U.S.C. § 4001(b).

[59] *See* 12 U.S.C. §§ 372, 635 a-4, 1841, 1843. Because Title II does not implicate the antitrust laws, it is not discussed further in these Guidelines.

[60] 15 U.S.C. §§ 4011-21.

[61] *Id.* § 6a (Sherman Act); *id.* § 45(a)(3) (FTC Act); *see infra* Sections 3.1-3.3.

[62] H.R. REP. NO. 97-924, at 26 (1982); *see* 15 U.S.C. § 4021(6).

[63] 15 U.S.C. § 4013(a).

The protections provided by an ETCR from the federal and state antitrust laws are not unlimited. First, conduct that falls outside the scope of a certificate remains fully subject to private and governmental enforcement actions. Second, an ETCR that is obtained by fraud is void from the outset and thus offers no protection under the antitrust laws. Third, any person that has been injured by certified conduct may recover actual (though not treble) damages if that conduct is found to violate any of the statutory criteria described above.[65] In any such action, certified conduct enjoys a presumption of legality, and the prevailing party is entitled to recover costs and attorneys' fees.[66] Fourth, an ETCR does not constitute, explicitly or implicitly, an endorsement or opinion by the Secretary of Commerce or by the Department concerning the legality of such business plans under the laws of any foreign country. Finally, an ETCR does not insulate conduct from investigation or enforcement by a foreign antitrust authority.

The Secretary of Commerce may revoke or modify an ETCR if the Secretary or the Department determines that the applicant's export activities have ceased to comply with the statutory criteria for obtaining a certificate.[67] The Department may also bring suit under Section 15 of the Clayton Act to enjoin conduct that threatens a "clear and irreparable harm to the national interest,"[68] even if the conduct has been pre-approved as part of an ETCR.

The Commerce Department, in consultation with the Department, has issued guidelines setting forth the standards used in reviewing ETCR applications.[69]

---

[64] H.R. REP. NO. 97-924, at 26(1982); *see* 15 U.S.C. § 4021(6).

[65] 15 U.S.C. § 4016(b)(1).

[66] *See id.* § 4016(b)(3), (b)(4).

[67] *Id.* § 4014(b).

[68] *Id.* § 4016(b)(5); *see also id.* § 25.

[69] *See* Int'l Trade Admin. (U.S. Dep't of Commerce), *The Export Trade Certificate of Review Program - The Competitive Edge for U.S. Exporters: Guidelines* (2015), http://trade.gov/mas/ian/etca/tg_ian_002140.asp. The Commerce Department's Export Trading Company Guidebook provides information on establishing and using an export trading company, including factors to consider when applying for an ETCR. Int'l Trade Admin. (U.S. Dep't of Commerce), *The Export Trading Company Guidebook* (1987). As of the date of these Guidelines, there are approximately 80 active certificates.

2.10 Wilson Tariff Act

The Wilson Tariff Act[70] prohibits "every combination, conspiracy, trust, agreement, or contract" made by or between two or more persons or corporations, either of whom is engaged in importing any article from a foreign country into the United States, where the agreement is intended to restrain trade or increase the market price in any part of the United States of the imported articles, or of "any manufacture into which such imported article enters or is intended to enter." Violation of the Wilson Tariff Act is a misdemeanor, punishable by a maximum fine of $5,000 or one year in prison. This Act also provides for seizure of the imported articles.[71]

2.11 Trade Act of 1974, Section 301

Section 301 of the Trade Act of 1974 provides that the U.S. Trade Representative ("USTR"), subject to the specific direction, if any, of the President, may take action, including restricting imports, to enforce rights of the United States under any trade agreement, to address acts inconsistent with the international legal rights of the United States, or to respond to unjustifiable, unreasonable or discriminatory practices of foreign governments that burden or restrict U.S. commerce.[72] Interested parties may initiate such actions through petitions to the USTR, or the USTR may itself initiate proceedings. Section 301(d)(3)(B)(i)(IV) includes the "toleration by a foreign government of systematic anticompetitive activities by enterprises or among enterprises in the foreign country that have the effect of restricting . . . access of United States goods or services to a foreign market" as one of the "unreasonable" practices that might justify such a proceeding.[73] The Department participates in the interagency committee that makes recommendations to the President on what actions, if any, should be taken.

2.12 Tariff Act of 1930

The Tariff Act of 1930[74] provides remedies for certain violations of the trade laws with antitrust implications, including violations of the laws regarding

---

[70] 15 U.S.C. §§ 8-11.

[71] *Id.* § 11.

[72] 19 U.S.C. § 2411.

[73] *Id.*

[74] *Id.*§§ 1202 *et seq.*

countervailing and anti-dumping duties.[75] Significant for purposes of the Agencies' enforcement of the federal antitrust laws, certain settlements of trade disputes entered under specific procedures set forth in the U.S. trade laws are granted implied immunity under this Act, even if the settlement involves price and quantity agreements or otherwise implicates the antitrust laws.[76] Agreements among competitors that do not comply with specific procedures in the U.S. trade laws or go beyond the measures authorized by such laws, however, are subject to the antitrust laws to the same extent as conduct unrelated to the settlement of a trade dispute. In the absence of legal authority, the fact, without more, that U.S. or foreign government officials were involved in or encouraged measures that would otherwise violate the antitrust laws does not immunize such arrangements.[77]

3. Agencies' Application of U.S. Antitrust Law to Conduct Involving Foreign Commerce

In making investigative and enforcement decisions, the Agencies focus on whether there is a sufficient connection between the anticompetitive conduct and the United States such that the federal antitrust laws apply and the Agencies' enforcement would redress harm or threatened harm to U.S. commerce and consumers. This Chapter describes circumstances under which a sufficient connection exists. If the Agencies determine that a sufficient connection exists, the Agencies generally will

---

[75] *Id.* §§ 1671, 1673.

[76] *See, e.g.*, Letter from Charles F. Rule, Acting Assistant Attorney General, Antitrust Division, Department of Justice, to Mr. Makoto Kuroda, Vice-Minister for International Affairs, Japanese Ministry of International Trade and Industry, July 30, 1986 (concluding that a suspension agreement did not violate the antitrust laws on the basis of factual representations that the agreement applied only to products under investigation, that it did not require pricing above levels needed to eliminate sales below foreign market value, and that assigning weighted-average foreign market values to exporters who were not respondents in the investigation was necessary to achieve the purpose of the anti-dumping law).

[77] *Cf. United States v. Socony-Vacuum Oil Co.*, 310 U.S. 150, 226 (1940) ("Though employees of the government may have known of those programs and winked at them or tacitly approved them, no immunity would have thereby been obtained. For Congress had specified the precise manner and method of securing immunity [in the National Industrial Recovery Act]. None other would suffice. . . ."); *see also Otter Tail Power Co. v. United States*, 410 U.S. 366, 378-79 (1973).

proceed in the normal course, subject to the considerations described in Chapter 4 and principles of prosecutorial discretion.

It is well established that the federal antitrust laws apply to foreign conduct that has a substantial and intended effect in the United States.[78] In 1982, Congress reaffirmed the applicability of the antitrust laws to conduct involving foreign commerce when it passed the FTAIA, which added Section 6a to the Sherman Act and Section 5(a)(3) to the FTC Act.[79] These provisions clarify whether the antitrust laws reach conduct—regardless of where it takes place—that involves trade or commerce with foreign nations.[80] Specifically, Section 6a provides:

> Sections 1 to 7 of [the Sherman Act] shall not apply to conduct involving trade or commerce (other than import trade or import commerce) with foreign nations unless—
>
> > (1) such conduct has a direct, substantial, and reasonably foreseeable effect—
> >
> > > (A) on trade or commerce which is not trade or commerce with foreign nations, or on import trade or import commerce with foreign nations; or

---

[78] *Hartford Fire Ins. Co. v. California*, 509 U.S. 764, 796 (1993); *United States v. Nippon Paper Indus. Co.*, 109 F.3d 1, 9 (1st Cir. 1997); *United States v. Aluminum Co. of Am.*, 148 F.2d 416, 444 (2d Cir. 1945).

[79] 15 U.S.C. § 6a (Sherman Act); *id.* § 45(a)(3) (FTC Act).

[80] The Supreme Court and other courts have declined to consider whether Section 6a amended existing law or merely codified it. *Hartford Fire*, 509 U.S. at 796 n.23; *Nippon Paper*, 109 F.3d at 4. Other courts have held that Section 6a supplanted the prior standard for the extraterritorial reach of the Sherman Act. *McGlinchy v. Shell Chem. Co.*, 845 F.2d 802, 813 n.8 (9th Cir. 1988); *The In Porters, S.A. v. Hanes Printables, Inc.*, 663 F. Supp. 494, 497 (M.D.N.C. 1987). If both the prior precedent and Section 6a apply in a single case, their requirements likely yield the same results. Conduct that either involves U.S. import commerce, *see infra* Section 3.1, or has a direct, substantial, and reasonably foreseeable effect on U.S. commerce, *see infra* Section 3.2, likely has a substantial and intended effect in the United States. In the Agencies' view, however, a separate showing of substantial and intended effects is unnecessary when some of the challenged conduct takes place in the United States because such a case would involve application, at least in part, of the U.S. antitrust law to territorial conduct.

(B) on export trade or export commerce with foreign nations, of a person engaged in such trade or commerce in the United States; and

(2) such effect gives rise to a claim under the provisions of sections 1 to 7 of this title, other than this section.

If sections 1 to 7 of this title apply to such conduct only because of the operation of paragraph (1)(B), then sections 1 to 7 of this title shall apply to such conduct only for injury to export business in the United States.[81]

Section 5(a)(3) of the FTC Act closely parallels this provision.[82]

Although the FTAIA clarified the reach of the Sherman Act and the FTC Act, it did not address the reach of the Clayton Act. Nevertheless, the Agencies would apply the principles outlined below when making enforcement decisions regarding mergers and acquisitions involving trade or commerce with foreign nations.

---

[81] 15 U.S.C. § 6a.

[82] *See* 15 U.S.C § 45(a)(3). The federal courts of appeals have expressed differing views as to whether the FTAIA goes to a claim's merits or a court's subject-matter jurisdiction. *Compare In re Monosodium Glutamate Antitrust Litig.*, 477 F.3d 535, 537 (8th Cir. 2007) (treating FTAIA as a question of subject-matter jurisdiction), *Empagran S.A. v. F. Hoffmann-LaRoche, Ltd.*, 417 F.3d 1267, 1269 (D.C. Cir. 2005) (same), *United States v. Anderson*, 326 F.3d 1319, 1329-30 (11th Cir. 2003) (same), *and Den Norske Stats Oljeselskap As v. HeereMac Vof*, 241 F.3d 420, 424-25 (5th Cir. 2001) (same), *with Minn-Chem, Inc. v. Agrium, Inc.*, 683 F.3d 845, 852 (7th Cir. 2012) (en banc) (FTAIA relates to merits of a claim), *overruling United Phosphorus, Ltd. v. Angus Chem. Co.*, 322 F.3d 942, 951-52 (7th Cir. 2003) (en banc) (FTAIA relates to court's subject-matter jurisdiction), *United States v. Hsiung*, 778 F.3d 738 (9th Cir. 2015) (merits), *overruling United States v. LSL Biotechs.*, 379 F.3d 672, 677 (9th Cir. 2004) (subject-matter jurisdiction), *Lotes Co., Ltd. v. Hon Hai Precision Indus. Co.*, 753 F.3d 395, 405 (2d Cir. 2014) (merits), *overruling Filetech S.A. v. France Telecom S.A.*, 157 F.3d 922, 929-32 (2d Cir. 1998) (subject-matter jurisdiction), and *Animal Sci. Prods., Inc. v. China Minmetals Corp.*, 654 F.3d 462, 467–68 (3d Cir. 2011) (merits), *overruling Carpet Grp. Int'l v. Oriental Rug Importers Ass'n, Inc.*, 227 F.3d 62, 69-70 (3d Cir. 2000) (subject-matter jurisdiction). This difference will not affect the Agencies' decisions about whether to proceed with an investigation or an enforcement action because the Agencies will not proceed when the FTAIA precludes the claim on the merits or strips the court of jurisdiction.

3.1 Conduct Involving Import Commerce

In general, the proscriptions in the Sherman Act and the FTC Act apply to conduct subject to Congress' constitutional power "to regulate commerce with foreign nations," among other things.[83] The FTAIA places "conduct involving trade or commerce (other than import trade or import commerce) with foreign nations" beyond the reach of these statutes, unless the conduct satisfies the FTAIA's effects exception described below.[84] The parenthetical language, however, excludes from the FTAIA's operation conduct involving import trade and import commerce. This provision is commonly referred to as the "import commerce exclusion."[85] As a result of this exclusion, conduct involving U.S. import commerce, like conduct involving commerce within the United States, is "subject to the Sherman Act's [or FTC Act's] general requirements for effects on commerce, not to the special requirements spelled out in the FTAIA."[86]

The import commerce exclusion does not apply to conduct merely because those participating in the conduct are also engaged in import commerce. Rather the conduct being challenged must itself involve import commerce.[87] Conversely, the import commerce exclusion may apply to conduct even if the participants themselves do not act as importers. For example, a firm cannot escape liability for unreasonably restraining or monopolizing import commerce by outsourcing the delivery of its product to the United States.

Conduct may "involve" import commerce even if it is not directed specifically or exclusively at import commerce and even if the import commerce involved

---

[83] U.S. Const. art. I, § 8, cl. 3; *see, e.g.,* 15 U.S.C. § 1 (outlawing conspiracies in unreasonably restraint of "trade or commerce . . . with foreign nations"); *id.* §§ 44, 45(a)(1) (outlawing "unfair methods of competition in or affecting" "commerce . . . with foreign nations"); *see generally United States v. Se. Underwriters Ass'n,* 322 U.S. 533, 588 (1944); *Fed. Trade Comm'n v. Klesner,* 274 U.S. 145, 151 (1927).

[84] *See infra* Section 3.2.

[85] *See, e.g., Minn-Chem,* 683 F.3d at 855.

[86] *Id.* at 854; *see Hsiung,* 778 F.3d at 754; *cf.* H.R. REP. No. 97-686, at 9 (1982) (explaining that "import restraints, which can be damaging to American consumers, remain covered by the law").

[87] *Carpet Grp.,* 227 F.3d at 71.

19

constitutes a relatively small portion of the worldwide commerce involved in the anticompetitive conduct.

Illustrative Example A

Situation: Corporation 1 and Corporation 2 have factories in Country Alpha where they manufacture Widget X. Corporation 1 and Corporation 2 agree to charge higher prices for Widget X. They sell Widget X to customers around the world, including in the United States.

Discussion: Corporation 1 and Corporation 2 manufacture Widget X outside the United States and sell Widget X in or for delivery to the United States. Thus their conspiracy to fix the price of Widget X is conduct involving U.S. import commerce. Accordingly, the conduct is prohibited by Section 1 of the Sherman Act as a conspiracy in restraint of "trade . . . with foreign nations," and Section 6a would not exempt this conspiracy from the antitrust laws. The circumstance that the price-fixing agreement concerned worldwide sales and did not specifically identify sales into the United States would not change the analysis. Likewise, even if the sales of Widget X in import commerce were a relatively small proportion or dollar amount of the price-fixed goods sold worldwide, the analysis would remain unchanged.[88]

Illustrative Example B

Situation: Shipping Corporation 1 and Shipping Corporation 2 are located in Country Alpha and provide international shipping services on various routes to the United States. Shipping Corporation 1 and Shipping Corporation 2 agree to charge higher prices for shipping services on select routes, including some routes to the United States.

Discussion: Shipping Corporation 1 and Shipping Corporation 2's conspiracy to fix the price of shipping services, which are closely connected to the importation of goods into the United States, is conduct involving import commerce. Moreover, the conduct would also involve

---

[88] *See generally Hsiung*, 778 F.3d at 754-56 (affirming Sherman Act convictions on ground that evidence that conspirators sold price-fixed components in or for delivery to the United States satisfied Section 6a's import commerce exclusion).

import commerce if Shipping Corporation 1 and Shipping Corporation 2 sold shipping services to customers in the United States for the transport of goods to the United States. In either case, the conduct is prohibited by Section 1 of the Sherman Act as a conspiracy in restraint of "trade . . . with foreign nations," and Section 6a would not exempt this conspiracy from the antitrust laws. The conduct also likely has a direct, substantial, and reasonably foreseeable effect on import commerce by raising the price of importing goods into the United States or of the imported goods themselves, in which case it would also satisfy the FTAIA's effects exception, described below.[89]

3.2 Conduct Involving Non-Import Foreign Commerce

The FTAIA initially places conduct involving non-import foreign commerce, which means U.S. export commerce and wholly foreign commerce, outside the reach of the Sherman Act and FTC Act.[90] What is commonly referred to as the FTAIA's "effects exception"[91] brings such conduct back within the reach of the Acts if the conduct has a direct, substantial, and reasonably foreseeable effect on commerce within the United States, U.S. import commerce, or the export commerce of a U.S. exporter, and that effect gives rise to a claim.[92]

Whether an alleged effect on such commerce is direct, substantial, and reasonably foreseeable is a question of fact. An effect on commerce is "direct" if there is a reasonably proximate causal nexus, that is, if the effect is proximately caused by the alleged anticompetitive conduct.[93] In other words, an effect is direct if, in the

---

[89] *See infra* Section 3.2.

[90] *F. Hoffmann-La Roche Ltd. v. Empagran S.A.*, 542 U.S. 155, 162-63 (2004).

[91] *See, e.g., Animal Sci. Prods., Inc. v. China Minmetals Corp.*, 654 F.3d 462, 471 (3d Cir. 2011).

[92] *Empagran*, 542 U.S. at 162.

[93] *See Minn-Chem*, 683 F.3d at 857; *Lotes Co. v. Hon Hai Precision Indus. Co.*, 753 F.3d 395, 409-13 (2d Cir. 2014). Although one court of appeals has held that an effect on U.S. commerce is "direct" for purposes of Section 6a only if it follows "as an immediate consequence" of the defendant's activity, *United States v. LSL Biotechs.*, 379 F.3d 672, 680 (9th Cir. 2004), the proximate cause standard is more consistent with the language of the statute. As the Seventh Circuit explained "[s]uperimposing

natural or ordinary course of events, the alleged anticompetitive conduct would produce an effect on commerce. The substantiality requirement does not provide a minimum pecuniary threshold, nor does it require that the effects be quantified.[94] Finally, the "reasonable foreseeability" requirement is an objective test, requiring that the effect be foreseeable to "a reasonable person making practical business judgments."[95]

Illustrative Example C

Situation: Corporation 1 and Corporation 2 have factories in Country Alpha where they manufacture Component X, a piece of high-tech hardware used in electronic products. Corporation 1 and Corporation 2 agree to raise prices for Component X sold to finished product integrators. These integrators have factories in Country Beta where they incorporate Component X into finished electronic products sold in the United States.

Discussion: Assuming Corporation 1 and Corporation 2 do not sell Component X in or for delivery to the United States, their conspiracy to fix the prices of Component X is conduct involving wholly foreign commerce, that is, commerce between Countries Alpha and Beta, and thus would not fall within the FTAIA's import commerce exclusion. The conduct would still fall within the reach of the Sherman Act if it has a (1) direct, (2) substantial, and (3) reasonably foreseeable effect on

---

the idea of 'immediate consequence' on top of the full [integrated] phrase ['direct, substantial, and reasonably foreseeable'] results in a stricter test than the complete text of the statute can bear" and "comes close to ignoring the fact that straightforward import commerce has already been excluded from the FTAIA's coverage." *Minn-Chem*, 683 F.3d at 857. Nevertheless, any difference between these two tests is unlikely to yield different results in the vast majority of cases.

[94] *Cf. McLain v. Real Estate Bd. of New Orleans, Inc.*, 444 U.S. 232, 243 (1980) ("Nor is jurisdiction defeated in a case relying on anticompetitive effects by plaintiff's failure to quantify the adverse impact of defendant's conduct."); *Goldfarb v. Va. State Bar*, 421 U.S. 773, 785 (1975) ("[O]nce an effect is shown, no specific magnitude need be proved").

[95] *Animal Sci.*, 654 F.3d at 471.

U.S. import commerce in finished electronic products that incorporate Component X.

Assessing the conduct's effects can be a fact-intensive inquiry. Here the Agencies would collect and analyze evidence to determine whether the price fixing of the component had an effect on U.S. import commerce. If it does, the Agencies would further analyze the evidence and collect additional evidence, as necessary, to determine: (1) whether the price fixing was the proximate cause of that effect, (2) whether the effect was substantial, and (3) whether that effect was a result of the price fixing that was foreseeable to a reasonable person making practical business judgments.

The fact that the price-fixed component was first sold to integrators in Country Beta, where it was incorporated into finished electronic products which were then sold in, or for delivery to, the United States would not render indirect an effect on import commerce in those products. Nor would the fact that the finished products were sold around the world or that Corporation 1 and Corporation 2 were unaware or indifferent to whether the finished products were sold in the United States render insubstantial or not reasonably foreseeable the effect on import commerce. In this context, substantiality is not a question of proportion. So long as the effect on import commerce is substantial, it does not matter if that effect is smaller than the conduct's effect outside the United States. Reasonable foreseeability is an objective standard, which asks not whether the conspirators actually foresaw the effect, but rather whether a reasonable person would foresee the effect on import commerce.

The relative size of Component X as a cost component of the finished electronic products may be relevant to determining whether the price-fixing conduct has the requisite effect, but it is not dispositive. For example, Component X may account for a large portion of the cost of the finished product, but competition from substitutes for the finished electronic products that do not incorporate Component X makes it unlikely that a price increase on Component X will affect import commerce in the finished products. Conversely, Component X may account for a small fraction of the cost of the finished product but the finished electronic product pricing is closely tied to input costs due to market conditions or contractual arrangements, or for other reasons. Thus, any price increase on Component X could, as a practical matter, have the requisite effect on import commerce in the finished electronic product.

Evidence that the conspirators actually expected their conduct to cause an effect on import commerce in the finished products would help to show that a direct, substantial, and reasonably foreseeable effect existed. Such evidence might include Corporation 1 and Corporation 2's contacts with purchasers in the United States, including negotiations regarding Component X pricing, as well as Corporation 1 and Corporation 2's discussing market conditions and tracking sales of the finished products in the United States. But the presence or absence of such evidence would not fundamentally alter the Agencies' analysis.[96]

Illustrative Example D

Situation: Company 1 and Company 2 are located in Country Alpha, where they extract Mineral X. Company 3 is located in the United States, where it extracts Mineral X. Company 3 is able to meet the entire U.S. demand for Mineral X and does so. Company 1 and Company 2 supply the rest of the world with Mineral X, but not the United States. By mutual agreement, Company 1 and Company 2 reduce their sales of Mineral X, significantly driving up the price of Mineral X outside the United States. Because of the increased price for Mineral X outside the United States, Company 3 begins to export much of the U.S. supply of Mineral X. No other firms replace Company 3's diverted sales, and the price of Mineral X rises inside the United States.

Discussion: Company 1 and Company 2's conspiracy to reduce their sales of Mineral X outside the United States is conduct involving wholly foreign commerce. Such conduct would fall within the reach of the Sherman Act if it has a direct, substantial, and reasonably foreseeable effect on U.S. interstate commerce in Mineral X. Here, the conspiracy had the effect of raising prices on interstate sales of Mineral

---

[96] *See generally Hsiung*, 778 F.3d at 756-60 (affirming Sherman Act convictions on alternate ground that evidence that price fixing of components sold abroad had a direct effect on U.S. import commerce in finished products containing price-fixed components satisfied Section 6a's effects exception).

X. That effect appears to be direct, substantial, and reasonably foreseeable.[97]

The FTAIA's effects exception also requires that the effect on commerce within the United States, U.S. import commerce, or the export commerce of a U.S. exporter "gives rise to" a claim under the antitrust laws. In a damages action brought under the antitrust laws, this provision requires that the effect on U.S. commerce be an adverse one and that the effect proximately cause the plaintiff's antitrust injury.[98] It is therefore appropriate for courts to distinguish among damages claims based upon the underlying transaction that forms the basis of the injury to ensure that each claim redresses injury consistent with the requirements of the antitrust laws, including the FTAIA. For example, when anticompetitive conduct affects commerce around the world, a plaintiff whose antitrust injury arises from that conduct's effect on U.S. import commerce may recover damages for that injury, but a plaintiff that suffers a foreign injury that is independent of, and not proximately caused by, the conduct's effect on U.S. commerce cannot recover damages under the U.S. antitrust laws.[99]

Similarly, when the United States is a plaintiff seeking damages under Section 4A of the Clayton Act for injury to its business or property, the United States must establish that the alleged conduct's effect on U.S. commerce proximately caused the injury to the United States' business or property.

---

[97] *Cf.* H.R. REP. NO. 97-686, at 13 (1982) ("For example, if a domestic export cartel were so strong as to have a 'spillover' effect on commerce within this country—by creating a world-wide shortage or artificially inflated world-wide price that had the effect of raising domestic prices—the cartel's conduct would fall within the reach of our antitrust laws. Such an impact would, at least over time, meet the test of a direct, substantial and reasonably foreseeable effect on domestic commerce.").

[98] *F. Hoffmann-La Roche Ltd. v. Empagran S.A.*, 542 U.S. 155, 173 (2004); *Lotes Co., Ltd. v. Hon Hai Precision Industry Co.*, 753 F.3d 395, 414 (2d Cir. 2014); *In re Dynamic Random Access Memory Antitrust Litig.*, 546 F.3d 981, 987 (9th Cir. 2008); *In re Monosodium Glutamate Antitrust Litig.*, 477 F.3d 535, 538 (8th Cir. 2007); *Empagran S.A. v. F. Hoffmann-La Roche Ltd.*, 417 F.3d 1267, 1271 (D.C. Cir. 2005).

[99] *Empagran*, 542 U.S. at 165, 169-73 (the federal antitrust laws "reflect a legislative effort to redress *domestic* antitrust injury that foreign anticompetitive conduct has caused") (emphasis added)); *see also Lotes*, 753 F.3d at 413-15.

Civil actions for equitable relief brought by the Agencies or criminal enforcement actions brought by the Department, on behalf of the United States, do not seek to redress a pecuniary injury to the government. Instead, such actions are brought by the sovereign to enjoin or prosecute a violation of its laws. In such cases, a direct, substantial, and reasonably foreseeable effect on U.S. commerce would give rise to the sovereign's claim.[100]

Thus, as a result of the effects exception's "gives rise to" provision, the Sherman Act can apply and not apply to the same conduct, depending upon the circumstances, including the plaintiff bringing the claim, the nature of the claim, and the injury underlying the claim.[101]

3.3 Conduct Involving U.S. Government Financing or Purchasing

The Agencies may, in appropriate cases, take enforcement action when the U.S. government is a purchaser, or substantially funds the purchase, of goods or services for consumption or use abroad. Cases in which the effect of anticompetitive conduct with respect to the sale of these goods or services falls primarily on U.S. taxpayers may qualify for redress under the federal antitrust laws.[102] The requisite U.S.

---

[100] The Department's Antitrust Corporate Leniency Policy requires applicants to make restitution to the victims of their offense. *See supra* n.42. Consistent with the Supreme Court's and courts of appeals' interpretation of the "gives rise to" provision that damages for violations of the Sherman Act are not available for foreign injuries independent of and not proximately caused by any adverse effect on U.S. commerce, *supra* n.98, the Department construes the leniency policy to not require restitution to victims whose antitrust injuries are independent of and not proximately caused by an adverse effect on (i) trade or commerce within the United States, (ii) import trade or commerce, or (iii) the export trade or commerce of a person engaged in such trade or commerce in the United States, which effect was proximately caused by the anticompetitive activity being reported.

[101] *Empagran*, 542 U.S. at 174; *see also Motorola Mobility LLC v. AU Optronics Corp.*, 775 F.3d 816, 820, 825 (7th Cir. 2014) (noting that the FTAIA "would not block the Department of Justice from seeking criminal or injunctive remedies" for price fixing that had the requisite effect on U.S. commerce, while holding private plaintiff could not recover damages because the injury did not arise from that effect).

[102] *See United States v. Anderson*, 326 F.3d 1319 (11th Cir. 2003) (applying Sherman Act to bid rigging on USAID-funded construction projects in Egypt). *Cf. United States v. Concentrated Phosphate Exp. Ass'n*, 393 U.S. 199, 208 (1968) ("[A]lthough the fertilizer shipments were consigned to Korea and although in most

government involvement could include an actual purchase of goods by the U.S. government for shipment abroad, a U.S. government grant to a foreign government that is specifically earmarked for the transaction, or a U.S. government loan specifically earmarked for the transaction that is made on such generous terms that it amounts to a grant. The Agencies consider U.S. government interests to be sufficiently affected when, as a result of its payment or financing, the U.S. government bears a substantial portion of the cost of the transaction. U.S. government interests would not be considered to be sufficiently implicated with respect to a transaction that is merely funded by an international agency, or a transaction in which the foreign government received non-earmarked funds from the United States as part of a general government-to-government aid program.

4. Agencies' Consideration of Foreign Jurisdictions

4.1 Comity

In enforcing the federal antitrust laws, the Agencies consider international comity. Comity itself reflects the broad concept of respect among co-equal sovereign nations and plays a role in determining "the recognition which one nation allows within its territory to the legislative, executive or judicial acts of another nation."[103] In determining whether to investigate or bring an action, or to seek particular remedies in a given case, the Agencies take into account whether significant interests of any foreign sovereign would be affected.[104]

---

cases Korea formally let the contracts, American participation was the overwhelmingly dominant feature. The burden of noncompetitive pricing fell, not on any foreign purchaser, but on the American taxpayer. The United States was, in essence, furnishing fertilizer to Korea. . . . The foreign elements in the transaction were, by comparison, insignificant."); *United States v. Standard Tallow Corp.*, No. 85-cv-2062, 1988 WL 72620 (S.D.N.Y. Jan. 28, 1988) (consent decree) (barring suppliers from fixing prices or rigging bids for the sale of tallow financed in whole or in part through grants or loans by the U.S. Government to the Government of Egypt); *United States v. Anthracite Exp. Ass'n*, No. 70-cv-9171, 1970 WL 540 (M.D. Pa. Nov. 12, 1970) (consent decree) (barring price-fixing, bid- rigging, and market allocation in Army foreign aid program).

[103] *Hilton v. Guyot*, 159 U.S. 113, 164 (1895).

[104] The Agencies, like other competition authorities around the world, consider the legitimate interests of foreign sovereigns in accordance with the recommendations

27

A decision to take an investigative step or to prosecute an antitrust action under the federal antitrust laws represents a determination that the importance of antitrust enforcement outweighs any relevant foreign policy concerns. That determination is entitled to deference.[105] Some courts have undertaken a comity analysis in disputes between private parties.[106]

In performing this comity analysis, the Agencies consider a number of relevant factors. The relative weight given to each factor depends on the facts and circumstances of each case. Among other things, the Agencies weigh: the existence of a purpose to affect or an actual effect on U.S. commerce; the significance and foreseeability of the effects of the anticompetitive conduct on the United States; the degree of conflict with a foreign jurisdiction's law or articulated policy; the extent to which the enforcement activities of another jurisdiction, including remedies resulting from those enforcement activities, may be affected; and the effectiveness of foreign enforcement as compared to U.S. enforcement.

An investigation or enforcement action by a foreign authority will not preclude an investigation or enforcement action by either the Department or the Commission. Rather, the Agency will determine whether, in light of actions by the foreign authority, investigation or enforcement is warranted to address harm or threatened harm to U.S. commerce and consumers from anticompetitive conduct. In cases in which an Agency opens an investigation or brings an enforcement action concerning conduct under investigation by a foreign authority, it may coordinate with that authority.[107]

Several of the comity factors considered by the Agencies warrant further discussion.

First, when considering the degree of conflict with foreign laws, the Agencies review the relevant laws of the interested foreign sovereigns. In the context of the Agencies' enforcement, conflicts of law are rare. As more jurisdictions have adopted and enforce antitrust laws that are compatible with those of the United States, it has

---

of the OECD and various bilateral agreements, and may, as appropriate, discuss these issues with foreign counterparts. *See infra* Chapter 5.

[105] *See, e.g., United States v. Baker Hughes, Inc.*, 731 F. Supp. 3, 6 n.5 (D.D.C.), *aff'd*, 908 F.2d 981 (D.C. Cir. 1990).

[106] *See, e.g., Timberlane Lumber Co. v. Bank of Am.*, 549 F.2d 597, 614-16 (9th Cir. 1976).

[107] *See infra* Chapter 5.

become increasingly common that no conflict exists between U.S. antitrust enforcement interests and the laws or policies of a foreign sovereign. Further, no conflict of law exists if a person subject to the laws of two sovereigns can comply with both.[108] Moreover, no conflict exists in cases where foreign law is neutral as to particular conduct, because it remains possible for the parties in question to comply with the U.S. antitrust laws without violating foreign law. In situations where a conflict of law exists, however, comity may counsel in favor of declining enforcement.

Second, the Agencies will assess the articulated interests and policies of a foreign sovereign beyond whether there is a conflict with foreign law. In determining whether to investigate or bring an enforcement action regarding an alleged antitrust violation, the Agencies consider the extent to which a foreign sovereign encourages or discourages certain courses of conduct or leaves parties free to choose among different courses of conduct.

Third, the Agencies consider whether the objectives sought to be obtained by U.S. enforcement could be achieved by foreign enforcement. The Agencies may consult with interested foreign authorities with the purpose of working to understand and address harm or threatened harm to U.S. commerce and consumers from anticompetitive conduct.

4.2 Consideration of Foreign Government Involvement

In some instances, a foreign government may be involved in anticompetitive conduct that involves or affects U.S. commerce. In determining whether to conduct an investigation or to file an enforcement action in cases in which foreign government involvement is known or suspected, the Agencies consider four legal doctrines that lie at the intersection of government action and the antitrust laws: (1) foreign sovereign immunity; (2) foreign sovereign compulsion; (3) act of state; and (4) petitioning of sovereigns.[109]

---

[108] *Hartford Fire Ins. Co. v. California*, 509 U.S. 764, 798-99 (1993).

[109] In some cases, investigation may be necessary to assess the nature of foreign government involvement and the applicability of the principles discussed below, even where an Agency ultimately refrains from enforcement.

4.2.1 Foreign Sovereign Immunity

In civil cases, the Foreign Sovereign Immunities Act of 1976 ("FSIA")[110] provides the "sole basis for obtaining jurisdiction over a foreign state in the courts of this country."[111] The FSIA shields foreign states[112] from the civil jurisdiction of the courts of the United States, subject to certain enumerated exceptions and to treaties in place at the time of the FSIA's enactment.[113] Under the FSIA, federal courts have jurisdiction over foreign states in certain cases in which the foreign state has:

    a. waived immunity explicitly or by implication;
    b. engaged in commercial activity;
    c. expropriated property in violation of international law;
    d. acquired rights to property in the United States;
    e. committed certain torts within the United States; or
    f. agreed to arbitration of the dispute.[114]

The "commercial activity" exception is the most relevant exception for antitrust purposes.[115] The FSIA provides that a foreign state is not immune from jurisdiction of U.S. courts when:

---

[110] 28 U.S.C. § 1330 *et seq.*

[111] *Argentine Republic v. Amerada Hess Shipping Corp.*, 488 U.S. 428, 443 (1989).

[112] The FSIA defines "foreign state" to include a "political subdivision of a foreign state or an agency or instrumentality of a foreign state." 28 U.S.C. § 1603(a). It further defines an "agency or instrumentality of a foreign state" to mean any entity "(1) which is a separate legal person, corporate or otherwise; and (2) which is an organ of a foreign state or political subdivision thereof, or a majority of whose shares or other ownership interest is owned by a foreign state or political subdivision thereof; and (3) which is neither a citizen of a State of the United States [as defined elsewhere in Title 28 of the U.S. Code], nor created under the laws of any third country." *Id.* § 1603(b). The majority-ownership prong of this definition encompasses state-owned corporations, so long as the "foreign state itself owns a majority of the corporation's shares." *Dole Food Co. v. Patrickson*, 538 U.S. 468, 477 (2003). The Act does not, however, apply to cases brought against individual foreign officials, whose immunity is governed instead by the common law. *Samantar v. Yousuf*, 560 U.S. 305, 319 (2010).

[113] 28 U.S.C. § 1604.

[114] *See generally id.* § 1605.

the action is based upon a commercial activity carried on in the United States by the foreign state; or upon an act performed in the United States in connection with a commercial activity of the foreign state elsewhere; or upon an act outside the territory of the United States in connection with a commercial activity of the foreign state elsewhere and that act causes a direct effect in the United States.[116]

"Commercial activity" is defined to include "either a regular course of commercial conduct or a particular commercial transaction or act," and the FSIA provides that "the commercial character of an activity shall be determined by reference to the nature of the course of conduct or particular transaction or act, rather than by reference to its purpose."[117] Commercial activity is distinct from sovereign activity inasmuch as the former is understood to include "those powers that can also be exercised by private citizens," while the latter is understood to include "powers peculiar to sovereigns."[118] In other words, the principal question is whether the government is acting "not as a regulator of a market, but in the manner of a private player within it."[119]

To determine whether an action is "based upon" a commercial activity, a court must focus on "the particular conduct on which the plaintiff's action is based," *i.e.*, "those

---

[115] *Id.* § 1605(a)(2); *see also id.* § 1603(e) (defining "commercial activity carried on in the United States by a foreign state" as "commercial activity carried on by such state and having substantial contact with the United States").

[116] *Id.* § 1605(a)(2).

[117] *Id.* § 1603(d).

[118] *Alfred Dunhill of London, Inc. v. Republic of Cuba*, 425 U.S. 682, 704 (1976).

[119] *Republic of Arg. v. Weltover, Inc.*, 504 U.S. 607, 614 (1992); *see also Saudi Arabia v. Nelson*, 507 U.S. 349, 360 (1993); *Universal Trading & Inv. Co. v. Bureau for Representing Ukrainian Interests in Int'l & Foreign Courts*, 727 F.3d 10, 19-20 (1st Cir. 2013); *Cmty. Fin. Grp., Inc. v. Republic of Kenya*, 663 F.3d 977, 980 (8th Cir. 2011); *Jurisdiction of U.S. Courts in Suits Against Foreign States: Hearings on H.R. 11315 Before Subcomm. on Admin. Law & Governmental Relations of the House Comm. on the Judiciary*, 94th Cong. 53 (1976) (statement of Monroe Leigh, Legal Advisor, U.S. Dep't of State) (courts should "inquire whether the activity in question is one which private parties ordinarily perform or whether it is peculiarly within the realm of governments").

elements that, if proven, would entitle a plaintiff to relief and the gravamen of the complaint."[120]

As a practical matter, most activities of foreign state-owned enterprises operating in the commercial marketplace are "commercial" and, therefore, such enterprises are not immune from the jurisdiction of the U.S. courts in actions to enforce the antitrust laws by virtue of the FSIA. The commercial activities of these enterprises are subject to the U.S. antitrust laws to the same extent as the activities of privately owned foreign firms.

4.2.2 Foreign Sovereign Compulsion

Because U.S. antitrust laws can extend to foreign persons and conduct with a sufficient connection to the United States, some persons may find themselves subject to foreign legal requirements that conflict with the laws of the United States. In these circumstances, courts have recognized a limited defense against application of the U.S. antitrust laws when a foreign sovereign compels the very conduct that the U.S. antitrust law would prohibit.[121] If it is possible, however, for a party to comply with both the foreign law and the U.S. antitrust laws, the existence of the foreign law does not provide any legal excuse for actions that do not comply with U.S. law.[122] Similarly, that conduct may be lawful, approved, or encouraged in a foreign jurisdiction does not, in and of itself, bar application of the U.S. antitrust

---

[120] *OBB Personenverkher AG v. Sachs*, 136 S. Ct. 390, 395 (2015) (citing *Saudi Arabia v. Nelson*, 507 U.S. 349, 356-57 (1993)) (internal quotation marks and alterations omitted).

[121] *See, e.g., Mannington Mills, Inc. v. Congoleum Corp.*, 595 F.2d 1287, 1293-94 (3d Cir. 1979); *Trugman-Nash, Inc. v. N.Z. Dairy Bd.*, 954 F. Supp. 733, 736 (S.D.N.Y. 1997); *Interamerican Refining Corp. v. Texaco Maracaibo, Inc.*, 307 F. Supp. 1291, 1304 (D. Del. 1970).

The defense of foreign sovereign compulsion is distinct from the state action doctrine articulated in *Parker v. Brown*, 317 U.S. 341 (1943). The state action doctrine applies to the actions of U.S. states and their subdivisions, and also to private anticompetitive conduct that is both: (1) undertaken pursuant to clearly articulated state policies and (2) actively supervised by the state. *See N.C. State Bd. of Dental Exam'rs v. Fed. Trade Comm'n*, 135 S. Ct. 1101 (2015).

[122] *Hartford Fire Ins. Co. v. California*, 509 U.S. 764, 798-99 (1993).

laws—even when the foreign jurisdiction has a strong policy in favor of the conduct in question.[123]

Two rationales underlie the limited defense of foreign sovereign compulsion. First, Congress enacted the U.S. antitrust laws against the background of well-recognized principles of international law and comity, pursuant to which U.S. authorities give due deference to the official acts of foreign governments. A defense for actions compelled by foreign sovereigns under certain circumstances serves to accommodate equal sovereigns. Second, fairness considerations require a mechanism to provide a predictable rule of decision for those seeking to conform their behavior to all applicable laws.

The Agencies recognize and consider this foreign sovereign compulsion defense when determining whether to bring an enforcement action. Because of the limited scope of the defense, however, the Agencies will refrain from bringing an enforcement action based on considerations of foreign sovereign compulsion only when certain criteria are satisfied.

First, the foreign government must have compelled the anticompetitive conduct under circumstances in which a refusal to comply with the foreign government's command would give rise to the imposition of penal or other severe sanctions. As a general matter, the Agencies regard the foreign government's formal representation that refusal to comply with its command would have such a result as being sufficient to establish that the conduct in question has been compelled. To be sufficient, however, the representation must contain enough detail to enable the Agencies to see precisely how the compulsion would be accomplished under foreign law.[124] Foreign government measures short of compulsion do not suffice for this defense, although they may be a relevant comity consideration if, for example, the measures reflect an articulated policy of the foreign government.

Second, the defense generally applies only when the compelled conduct can be accomplished entirely within the foreign sovereign's own territory. If the compelled

---

[123] *Id.* Discretionary conduct is also outside the protections afforded by this defense. *See Continental Ore Co. v. Union Carbide & Carbon Corp.*, 370 U.S. 690, 706-07 (1962).

[124] For example, the Agencies may not regard as dispositive a statement that is unsupported or ambiguous, or that, on its face, appears to be internally inconsistent. The Agencies may inquire into the circumstances underlying the statement and may request further information if the source of the power to compel is unclear.

conduct occurs in the United States, the Agencies will not recognize the defense.[125] For example, the defense would not apply if a foreign government required the U.S. subsidiaries of several firms to organize a cartel in the United States to fix the price at which products would be sold in the United States.

Third, the order must come from the foreign government acting in its governmental capacity.[126] The defense does not arise from conduct that would fall within the FSIA commercial activity exception.

Illustrative Example E

Situation: Increased quantities of Commodity X have flooded the world market over the last several years, including substantial amounts coming into the United States. The officials of Countries Alpha, Beta, and Gamma meet with their respective domestic firms and urge them to "rationalize" production of Commodity X by cooperatively cutting back. Going one step further, the government of Country Gamma orders cutbacks from its domestic firms, subject to substantial penalties for non-compliance. Producers from Countries Alpha and Beta agree among themselves to institute comparable cutbacks, but their governments do not require them to do so. The overseas production cutbacks have sufficient effects on U.S. commerce for the antitrust laws to apply.

Discussion: The Agencies would not find that foreign sovereign compulsion precludes prosecution of the agreement in restraint of trade entered into by the participants from Countries Alpha and Beta.[127] The Agencies would acknowledge a defense of sovereign compulsion, however, for the participants from Country Gamma.

---

[125] *See Linseman v. World Hockey Ass'n*, 439 F. Supp. 1315, 1324-25 (D. Conn. 1977).

[126] *See supra* Section 4.2.1.

[127] As in all such cases, the Agencies would also consider whether comity factors counsel against bringing an enforcement action for the conduct. *See supra* Section 4.1.

4.2.3 Act of State Doctrine

The act of state doctrine prevents courts from "declar[ing] invalid the official act of a foreign sovereign performed within its own territory."[128] Applying this doctrine, courts decline to adjudicate claims or issues that would require the court to judge the validity of the sovereign act of a foreign state in its own territory.[129] This doctrine is rooted in considerations of international comity and the separation of powers.[130]

The doctrine does not apply to every act taken by an individual or entity affiliated with a sovereign state. For instance, it does not apply to the acts of individual government officials acting outside their official capacity.[131] Nor does it apply to private actors, even when those acts are approved or condoned by the foreign government in question.[132]

Accordingly, when a restraint on competition arises directly from the act of a foreign sovereign, such as the grant of a license, award of a contract, or expropriation of property, the Agencies may refrain from bringing an enforcement action based on the principles animating the act of state doctrine. More specifically, the Agencies may exercise enforcement discretion and decline to challenge foreign acts of state if

---

[128] *W.S. Kirkpatrick & Co. v. Envt'l Tectonics Corp., Int'l*, 493 U.S. 400, 405 (1990); *Banco Nacional de Cuba v. Sabbatino*, 376 U.S. 398, 401 (1964); *Underhill v. Hernandez*, 168 U.S. 250, 252 (1897) ("Every sovereign state is bound to respect the independence of every other sovereign state, and the courts of one country will not sit in judgment on the acts of the government of another, done within its own territory. Redress of grievances by reason of such acts must be obtained through the means open to be availed of by sovereign powers as between themselves.").

[129] *See W.S. Kirkpatrick*, 493 U.S. at 406 ("Act of state issues only arise when a court *must decide*—that is, when the outcome of the case turns upon—the effect of official action by a foreign sovereign. When that question is not in the case, neither is the act of state doctrine.").

[130] *Id.* at 404; *Sabbatino*, 376 U.S. at 423 (the doctrine "express[es] the strong sense of the Judicial Branch that its engagement in the task of passing on the validity of foreign acts of state may hinder rather than further this country's pursuit of goals . . . in the international sphere").

[131] *Republic of Iraq v. ABB AG*, 768 F.3d 145, 165 (2d Cir. 2014).

[132] *See, e.g., In re Potash Antitrust Litig.*, 686 F. Supp. 2d 816, 825 (N.D. Ill. 2010).

the facts and circumstances indicate that: (1) the specific conduct complained of is a public act of the sovereign, (2) the act was taken within the territorial jurisdiction of the sovereign, and (3) the conduct relates to a matter that is governmental, rather than commercial.[133]

4.2.4 Petitioning of Sovereigns

Under the *Noerr-Pennington* doctrine, a genuine effort to obtain or influence action by governmental entities in the United States falls outside the scope of the Sherman Act, even if the intent or effect of that effort is to restrain or monopolize trade.[134] It is the view of the Agencies that the principles undergirding this doctrine apply to the petitioning of foreign governments. The Agencies, therefore, will not challenge under the antitrust laws genuine efforts to obtain or influence action by foreign government entities.[135] But as with *Noerr-Pennington*, the Agencies will not exercise this discretion when faced with "sham" activities, in which petitioning "ostensibly directed toward influencing governmental action, is a mere sham to cover . . . an attempt to interfere directly with the business relationships of a competitor,"[136] or when *Noerr-Pennington* would otherwise not apply.[137]

Illustrative Example F

Situation: Corporation 1 and Corporation 2 have mines in Country Alpha where they extract Mineral X. Corporation 1 and Corporation 2

---

[133] *See Alfred Dunhill of London, Inc. v. Republic of Cuba,* 425 U.S. 682, 704 (1976) (plurality op. of White, J.). *Cf. supra* Section 4.2.1.

[134] *See United Mine Workers of Am. v. Pennington,* 381 U.S. 657 (1965); *E.R.R. Presidents Conference* v. *Noerr Motor Freight, Inc.,* 365 U.S. 127 (1961); *see also Cal. Motor Transp. Co. v. Trucking Unlimited,* 404 U.S. 508 (1972) (extending protection to petitioning before "all departments of Government," including the courts).

[135] *Cf. Amarel v. Connell,* 102 F.3d 1494, 1520 (9th Cir. 1996).

[136] *Prof'l Real Estate Investors, Inc. v. Columbia Pictures Indus.,* 508 U.S. 49, 56 (1993) (internal quotations omitted).

[137] *See, e.g., Allied Tube & Conduit Corp. v. Indian Head, Inc.,* 486 U.S. 492 (1988); *Walker Process Equip., Inc. v. Food Mach. & Chem. Corp.,* 382 U.S. 172 (1965).

use different techniques to extract Mineral X. Corporation 1 launches a campaign designed to foster the adoption and retention of regulations that would effectively outlaw Corporation 2's mining technique. As part of this broader campaign, Corporation 1 files a complaint with Country Alpha's Ministry of Mines alleging severe health and safety concerns stemming from Corporation 2's mining technique and demanding the permanent closure of Corporation 2's mine. If successful, Corporation 1 would have an effective monopoly on the U.S. market for Mineral X. The Country Alpha Ministry of Mines decides to investigate the complaint, leading to the temporary shutdown of Corporation 2's operations.

Discussion: Had Corporation 1's activities been directed at a U.S. government entity and the *Noerr-Pennington* doctrine applied, the Agencies would not take action against Corporation 1. Applying like principles here, the Agencies would not institute enforcement action against Corporation 1 for lodging a complaint with the Country Alpha Ministry of Mines.

5. International Cooperation

Effective enforcement of the U.S. antitrust laws in a global economy benefits from cooperation with foreign authorities. The Agencies are committed to cooperating with foreign authorities on both policy and investigative matters. This cooperation contributes to convergence on substantive enforcement standards that seek to advance consumer welfare, based on sound economics, procedural fairness, transparency, and non-discriminatory treatment of parties. The Agencies' international policy work and case cooperation are closely connected. As noted above, consistent approaches to competition law, policy, and procedures across jurisdictions facilitate case cooperation among competition authorities. Moreover, through case cooperation, the Agencies and cooperating authorities often raise important substantive and procedural issues as they arise in practice, which can lead to greater convergence in substantive analysis and procedures. In keeping with these Guidelines' focus on international enforcement and practice, this Chapter focuses on investigations and case cooperation.

International case cooperation helps agencies investigating a particular matter to identify issues of common interest, gain a better understanding of relevant facts, and achieve consistent outcomes. Cooperation can yield better results for competition and promote efficiency for both cooperating agencies and subjects of an investigation. It can improve substantive analyses and procedures, and ensure that investigations and remedies are as consistent and predictable as possible, which improves outcomes, and reduces uncertainty and expense to firms doing business across borders. When either Agency reviews a case that raises possible competitive concerns in jurisdictions outside of the United States, it may consult with the relevant foreign authorities about the matter and coordinate and cooperate with those authorities conducting parallel investigations.[138] As described in greater detail throughout this chapter, cooperation can include a broad range of practices, from initiating informal discussions and informing cooperating authorities of the different stages of their investigations, to engaging in detailed discussions of substantive issues, exchanging information, conducting interviews at which two or more agencies may be present, and coordinating remedy design and implementation, as relevant and appropriate.[139]

5.1 Investigations and Cooperation

Increasingly, the Agencies' investigations involve conduct, entities, individuals, and information located outside the United States. The Agencies employ a combination of their own investigative tools and cooperation with foreign authorities in investigating and seeking appropriate remedies in certain international matters.

5.1.1 Investigative Tools

When practical and consistent with enforcement objectives, the Agencies may request that parties and third parties voluntarily: provide documents; submit to interviews; or provide other information related to an investigation. These requests may seek documents or information located outside the United States.

The Agencies also may use compulsory measures to obtain documents and information. Specifically, the Agencies may compel production of documents or

---

[138] An Agency may continue that cooperation when either it or the foreign authority has closed its investigation. The Agencies may also engage in general discussions with foreign authorities on matters in which only one authority has an open investigation.

[139] The Agencies do not conduct "joint investigations" with foreign authorities; neither Agency exercises control over foreign authorities regarding their investigations, nor accepts direction from foreign authorities regarding its own investigations. The Agencies, however, do cooperate with foreign authorities conducting parallel investigations. "[R]obust information-sharing and cooperation across parallel investigations" do not transform multiple parallel investigations into a joint investigation. *United States v. Getto*, 729 F.3d 221, 231 (2d Cir. 2013).

information via civil investigative demand ("CID") or subpoena.[140] U.S. law provides authority for such compulsory measures directed to persons over whom the courts have personal jurisdiction.[141] The Agencies may compel the production of documents or information, including documents or information located outside the United States, when the documents or information sought are within the "possession, custody, or control" of an individual or entity subject to the jurisdiction of the United States and are not protected by the attorney-client privilege or the work-product doctrine.[142]

When one of the Agencies investigates a transaction notified under the HSR Act, it may issue a request for additional documents or information, typically called a "Second Request."[143] Compliance with a Second Request requires production of all responsive documents and information, no matter where located.

Conflicts can arise where foreign statutes purport to prevent individuals or entities from disclosing documents or information for use in U.S. proceedings. The mere existence of such statutes, however, does not excuse noncompliance with a request for documents or information from one of the Agencies.[144]

---

[140] The Department may issue CIDs pursuant to the Antitrust Civil Process Act, 15 U.S.C.§ 1312, and the FTC may issue CIDs and subpoenas pursuant to the FTC Act. *Id.* §§ 49, 57b-1(c). In merger investigations, the Agencies utilize the mechanisms of the HSR Act to gather information from parties. *Id.* § 18(a). *See also* U.S. Dep't of Justice, *Crim. Resource Manual* § 279 (discussing availability of subpoenas reaching individuals and evidence located abroad), https://www.justice. gov/usam/criminal-resource-manual-279-subpoenas.

[141] *In re Grand Jury Proceedings (Bank of Nova Scotia)*, 740 F.2d 817, 828-29 (11th Cir. 1984); *United States v. First Nat'l City Bank*, 396 F.2d 897, 900-901 (2d Cir. 1968); *see also, e.g.*, 28 U.S.C. § 1783(a) (authorizing a U.S. court to order the issuance of a subpoena "requiring the appearance as a witness before it, or before a person or body designated by it, of a national or resident of the United States who is in a foreign country, or requiring the production of a specified document or other thing by him," under circumstances identified in the statute).

[142] 15 U.S.C. § 57b-1(c)(1) (FTC Act); *id.* § 1312(a) (Antitrust Civil Process Act).

[143] See Section 2.2.4, *supra*, regarding the HSR Act.

[144] The Agencies do not view the mere existence of blocking statutes as creating a conflict of law for purposes of the comity analysis. *Cf. Société Nationale Industrielle*

Because unilaterally collecting documents or information from individuals or entities located abroad can adversely affect law enforcement relationships with foreign countries, the Agencies use compulsory measures after carefully considering the importance of the documents or information to the investigation or prosecution and the availability of other means to obtain them.[145] When such compulsory measures are warranted, the Agencies may seek to work with the foreign authority involved as appropriate.

5.1.2 Confidentiality

The Agencies' enforcement activities benefit greatly from access to sensitive, nonpublic information from businesses and consumers. The Agencies recognize the importance of protecting the confidentiality of sensitive, nonpublic information received from parties and foreign authorities. The Agencies protect the confidentiality of all such information received, be it from businesses or consumers located domestically or abroad, or from foreign authorities, under applicable provisions of U.S. law.

Several statutes require the Agencies to treat as confidential certain information obtained in the course of an investigation. The HSR Act prohibits the Agencies from disclosing information obtained pursuant to the act, including the fact that the parties filed notice of a proposed transaction and confidential business information provided in a filing or in response to a document or information request.[146] The FTC Act restricts disclosure of information that the Commission receives pursuant to compulsory process, or produced voluntarily in lieu of process, in a law enforcement investigation.[147] The FTC Act also prohibits the Commission from making public any trade secret or any commercial or financial information it obtains that is

---

Aérospatiale v. U.S. Dist. Court, 482 U.S. 522, 542-44 & n. 29 (1987). Comity is addressed in Section 4.1.

[145] U.S. Dep't of Justice, *Crim. Resource Manual* § 279, https://www.justice.gov/usam/criminal-resource-manual-279-subpoenas.

[146] *See* 15 U.S.C. § 18a(h).

[147] 15 U.S.C. §§ 57b-2(b), 57b-2(f). Section 21(f) of the FTC Act also explicitly protects from disclosure any materials received from a non-U.S. competition authority when "the foreign law enforcement agency or other foreign government agency has requested confidential treatment, or has precluded such disclosure under other use limitations, as a condition of providing the material." *Id.* § 57b-2(f).

privileged or confidential, except in limited circumstances.[148] The Antitrust Civil Process Act prohibits the Department from disclosing documents or testimony obtained pursuant to a CID without the consent of the person that produced the materials, except in limited circumstances.[149] Other federal laws also require the Agencies to treat specific types of information as confidential, without regard to the manner in which the information is obtained. For example, laws governing privacy, national security information, and trade secrets require that the Agencies treat certain information as confidential.[150]

There are certain, discrete circumstances in which the Agencies may disclose a person's confidential information for a specific use. The HSR Act, the FTC Act, and the Antitrust Civil Process Act do not bar the Agencies' use of a person's confidential information in judicial and administrative proceedings.[151] However, the Federal Rules of Civil Procedure and FTC Rules of Practice include procedures to protect confidential information used in judicial proceedings or FTC administrative proceedings.[152]

The Agencies also are subject to the Freedom of Information Act ("FOIA"), which provides the public with a right of access to certain agency records.[153] This statute, however, contains several exemptions that protect information provided to the Agencies. It permits the Agencies to withhold certain categories of documents from

---

[148] *Id.* § 46(f).

[149] *See* 15 U.S.C. § 1313(c)(2), (d).

[150] For example, U.S. law imposes confidentiality obligations regarding certain classes of information, including personally identifiable information. *See, e.g.* 5 U.S.C. § 552a (Privacy Act of 1974).

[151] In addition, the FTC Act, with regard to the Commission, and HSR Act do not prevent the Agencies from complying with information requests from Congress. In the event of such a request, however, the Agency receiving the request must notify the submitter of the information, and the Agency can request confidential treatment of any information that may be shared.

[152] For instance, the person providing information may seek a protective order to prevent confidential information from being made public or from being used outside the court proceeding. *See* Fed. R. Civ. P. 26(c); 16 C.F.R. § 3.31(d) (requiring Administrative Law Judge in FTC proceeding to issue a specific protective order).

[153] 5 U.S.C. § 552.

requesters, including information protected by statute (such as the HSR Act or FTC Act), "commercial or financial information obtained from a person [that is] privileged or confidential," inter- or intra-agency memoranda or letters that would be routinely privileged in civil discovery, and "files the disclosure of which would constitute a clearly unwarranted invasion of personal privacy."[154] In addition, an exemption from FOIA's disclosure regime applies to certain information compiled for law enforcement purposes, including when disclosure could interfere with enforcement proceedings or disclose the identity of a confidential source.[155]

5.1.3 Legal Bases for Cooperation

The Agencies' authority to cooperate with foreign authorities is inherent in their ability to act in furtherance of their mandates. The Department and FTC, therefore, each has the discretion to cooperate, including when it furthers its enforcement interests. Cooperation can be facilitated by bilateral and multilateral arrangements.[156] The Agencies have also developed best practices and guidance documents on cooperation for specific types of investigations.[157] These

---

[154] *Id.* § 552(b)(3)-(6).

[155] *Id.* § 552(b)(7).

[156] For example, the United States or the Agencies have bilateral cooperation agreements with eleven jurisdictions or competition agencies: Germany (1976); Australia (1982); the European Union (1991); Canada (1995); Brazil, Israel, and Japan (1999); Mexico (2000); Chile (2011); Colombia (2014); and Peru (2016). The Agencies also have entered into memoranda of understanding with the Russian Federal Antimonopoly Service (2009), the three Chinese antimonopoly enforcement agencies (2011), the Indian competition authorities (2012), and the Korea Fair Trade Commission (2015). These arrangements are available at https://www. justice.gov/atr/antitrust-cooperation-agreements and https://www.ftc.gov/policy/ international/international-cooperation-agreements. Multilateral arrangements include the Recommendation of the OECD Council Concerning Co-Operation on Competition Investigations and Proceedings, and the ICN Framework for Merger Cooperation. Org. for Econ. Co-Operation & Dev., Recommendation of the OECD Council Concerning Co-Operation on Competition Investigations and Proceedings (2014), http://www.oecd.org/competition/international-coop-competition-2014-recommendation.htm; Int'l Competition Network, Framework for Merger Cooperation (2012), http://www.internationalcompetitionnetwork.org/uploads/ library/doc803.pdf.

[157] *See, e.g.*, US-EU Merger Working Grp., *Best Practices on Cooperation in Merger Investigations* (2011), https://www.justice.gov/atr/best-practices-cooperation-merger-

arrangements and guidance documents can serve as a catalyst for cooperation and provide useful guidance to coordinate and facilitate enforcement activities. They are not necessary for cooperation to take place, and the Agencies may cooperate with relevant foreign authorities in the absence of any formal arrangement. These bilateral and multilateral arrangements do not change the signatories' laws, including laws concerning the treatment of confidential information.

The IAEAA authorizes the Agencies to enter into antitrust-specific mutual assistance agreements with foreign authorities that allow the Agencies to share evidence relating to antitrust violations already in their possession and provide each other with investigatory assistance in obtaining evidence, subject to certain limitations.[158] As noted in Section 2.6, the IAEAA does not apply to materials submitted pursuant to the HSR Act.[159]

---

investigations; China Ministry of Comm., Fed. Trade Comm'n, U.S. Dep't of Justice, *Guidance for Case Cooperation between the Ministry of Commerce and the Department of Justice and Federal Trade Commission on Concentration of Undertakings (Merger) Cases* (2011), https://www.ftc.gov/system/files/attachments/press-releases/federal-trade-commission-department-justice-meet-chinese-ministry-commerce-merger-enforcement/111129mofcom.pdf; U.S.- Can. Working Grp., *Best Practices on Cooperation in Merger Investigations* (2014), https://www.justice.gov/sites/default/files/atr/legacy/2014/03/25/304654.pdf; Int'l Competition Network, *Anti-Cartel Enforcement Manual*, http://www.international competitionnetwork.org/working-groups/current/cartel/manual.aspx; Int'l Competition Network, *Recommended Practices for Merger Notification and Review Procedures*, http://www.internationalcompetitionnetwork.org/uploads/library/doc588.pdf; Int'l Competition Network, *Recommended Practices for Merger Analysis*, http://www.internationalcompetitionnetwork.org/uploads/library/doc316.pdf; Int'l Competition Network, *Practical Guide to Enforcement Cooperation in Mergers*, http://www.internationalcompetitionnetwork.org/uploads/library/doc1031.pdf; Org. for Econ. Co-Operation & Development, *Best Practices for Formal Exchange of Information Between Competition Authorities in Hard Core Cartel Investigations* (2005), http://www.oecd.org/competition/cartels/35590548.pdf.

[158] 15 U.S.C. § 6201 *et seq.*, discussed *supra* Section 2.6. Mutual Legal Assistance Treaties may be used in the criminal context, discussed *infra* Section 5.2.

[159] *Id.* § 6204(1).

5.1.4 Types of Information Exchanged and Waivers of Confidentiality

If a transaction or conduct under antitrust investigation in the United States is also being investigated by a foreign authority, the Department or the Commission may contact the authority. The Agencies may share with these foreign authorities relevant publicly available information.[160] Similarly, it remains in the Agencies' discretion whether to share with cooperating foreign authorities agency non-public information, which is information that the Agencies are not statutorily prohibited from disclosing, but that the Agencies normally treat as non-public and withhold from public disclosure.[161] Examples of agency non-public information include the existence of an open investigation and the Agencies' staff views as to the merits of a case, market definition, competitive effects, substantive theories of harm, and remedies. Before exchanging agency non-public information, the Agencies will have reached an understanding that the foreign authority will maintain the information in confidence and in accordance with that authority's laws and rules. This may be through bilateral or multilateral cooperation agreements or arrangements, or other means.

While confidentiality obligations generally prohibit the Agencies from disclosing to foreign authorities confidential information submitted by a person,[162] that person can enable the Agencies to engage in more meaningful cooperation with foreign authorities by granting the Agencies a waiver of confidentiality as to information that may be otherwise protected from disclosure. The Agencies issued a joint model waiver of confidentiality for use in civil matters, which serves to streamline the waiver process[163] and published explanatory materials that provide further details on waivers of confidentiality, applicable confidentiality rules, and the process for providing a waiver of confidentiality.[164]

---

[160] The types of relevant publicly available information that the Agencies may share with foreign authorities include background information regarding a particular industry or company and public records, such as court or securities filings.

[161] *See, e.g.,* 5 U.S.C. § 552(b)(5).

[162] *See supra* Section 5.1.2.

[163] Fed. Trade Comm'n & Dep't of Justice, *Model Waiver of Confidentiality* (2013), https://www.ftc.gov/sites/default/files/attachments/international-waivers-confidentiality-ftc-antitrust-investigations/model_waiver.pdf.

[164] U.S. Dep't of Justice & Fed. Trade Comm'n, *Model Waiver of Confidentiality for Use in Civil Matters Involving Non-U.S. Competition Auths. Frequently Asked*

A waiver identifies the terms under which a person agrees to waive statutory confidentiality protections vis-à-vis the agency that originally received the person's confidential information. A waiver also describes an agency's policy regarding how it will treat the information it receives from another agency pursuant to a waiver, although it is not an agreement signed by the agency. Waivers are limited in scope to a specific, named matter and designate the agencies that may share the waiving person's confidential information. Waivers generally allow the cooperating authorities to share documents, statements, data, and other information.

Waivers enable deeper communication, cooperation, and coordination among competition authorities concurrently reviewing a matter. They can lead to more effective, efficient investigations and better-informed, more consistent enforcement decisions based on the Agencies' increased ability to share information.

The Agencies will protect information received from a foreign authority pursuant to a waiver under applicable provisions of U.S. law. The Agencies will not seek information that is privileged under U.S. law from foreign authorities through waivers or other cooperative activities.[165]

Similarly, the Agencies will provide information to foreign authorities pursuant to a waiver when they have reached an understanding with the recipient agency that it will maintain the confidentiality of such information consistent with its laws and rules. Generally, a person that has waived the confidentiality of its information as to one of the Agencies also will provide a separate waiver of confidentiality to the relevant foreign authority, based on the waiving person's understanding of the foreign authority's confidentiality protections.

The Agencies may request a waiver of confidentiality, but the decision whether to provide one rests solely with the producing person. Refusal to provide a waiver will not prejudice the outcome of an investigation, though, in some cases, the absence of a waiver may have practical effects such as increasing the risk of inconsistent outcomes between jurisdictions. Further, declining to grant a waiver will not preclude the Agencies from sharing publicly available or agency non-public information with foreign authorities.

Questions (2015), www.justice.gov/sites/default/files/atr/legacy/2015/05/11/300916.pdf.

[165] *Id.*

Illustrative Example G

Situation: Corporation 1 and Corporation 2 each manufacture Product X and Product Y. Corporation 1 and Corporation 2 enter into an agreement to merge. The proposed merger meets the threshold for premerger notification in the United States under the HSR Act and the thresholds for premerger notification in several other jurisdictions. Corporation 1 and Corporation 2 inform the U.S. Agency reviewing the merger as well as reviewing foreign authorities that the merger will be notified or reviewed in multiple jurisdictions. Pre-notification consultations and pre-merger filings are timed to facilitate communication and cooperation among reviewing authorities at key decision-making stages of their respective investigations.

Discussion: After learning that the merger will be notified or reviewed in more than one jurisdiction, the U.S. Agency contacts the foreign reviewing authorities to discuss review timetables and assess the potential for cooperation. The extent of cooperation with each foreign authority reviewing the matter will vary depending on factors including the depth of that authority's investigation, the competitive conditions in that authority's jurisdiction, and the scope of potential remedies likely to be considered. The U.S. Agency requests a waiver of confidentiality from Corporation 1 and Corporation 2 to allow for the exchange of confidential information with the reviewing authorities in Countries Alpha, Beta, and Gamma, given the nature of the competitive concerns raised by the merger in these jurisdictions. Corporation 1 and Corporation 2 voluntarily grant these waivers, as well as the waivers of confidentiality requested by each of these reviewing authorities. The U.S. Agency cooperates with the reviewing authorities in Countries Delta and Epsilon on the basis of publicly available and agency non-public information, without exchanging confidential business information.

As reviews of the merger proceed, the U.S. Agency and the other reviewing authorities arrange communications between and among themselves as appropriate to their investigations. The U.S. Agency and authorities of Alpha, Beta, and Gamma each arrange regular, bilateral calls and, in some instances, certain of these agencies conduct interviews together, facilitated by waivers. These reviewing agencies, as well as the reviewing authorities of Delta and Epsilon, also conduct status calls, based on publicly available and agency non-public information to update each other on the timing of reviews and theories of harm. The reviewing authorities of Delta and Epsilon identify that the merger's effects in their jurisdictions are likely to be insignificant, and that they will close their investigations accordingly.

5.1.5 Remedies

The Agencies seek remedies that effectively address harm or threatened harm to U.S. commerce and consumers, while attempting to avoid conflicts with remedies contemplated by their foreign counterparts.[166] An Agency will seek a remedy that includes conduct or assets outside the United States only to the extent that including them is needed to effectively redress harm or threatened harm to U.S. commerce and consumers[167] and is consistent with the Agency's international comity analysis.[168]

When multiple authorities are investigating the same transaction or same conduct, the Agencies may cooperate with other authorities, to the extent permitted under

---

[166] *United States v. General Elec. Co. et al.*, No. 15-cv-1460 (D.D.C. 2015); *In re Panasonic Corp. et al*, Dkt. No. C-4274 (FTC Jan. 8, 2010) (allowed for extension of divestiture deadline if necessary to obtain approval for divestiture from the European Commission).

[167] *Polypore Int'l, Inc. v. Fed. Trade Comm'n*, 686 F.3d 1208, 1219 (11th Cir. 2012) (affirming Commission decision in a merger matter with remedy including assets located outside the United States); *United States. v. Cont'l AG & Veyance Technologies*, No. 14-cv-2087 (D.D.C. 2014) (facilities in Mexico divested); *U.S. v. Anheuser-Busch InBev SA/NV & Grupo Modelo S.A.B. DE C.V.*, No. 13-cv-127 (D.D.C 2013) (brewery in Mexico divested); *In re Victrex, plc*, Dkt. No. C–4586 (FTC July 14, 2016) (remedy prohibiting contract provisions that could result in exclusivity, including when products are manufactured or sold abroad for use in products sold or cleared for use in the United States); *In re Intel Corp.*, Dkt. No. 9341 (FTC Nov. 2, 2010) (remedy including requirements regarding licensing with foreign CPU maker that potentially competed with Intel in order to restore competition in United States). These remedies are often entered into voluntarily pursuant to consent decrees.

[168] *See supra* Section 4.1.

U.S. law, to facilitate obtaining effective and non-conflicting remedies.[169] Cooperation also may facilitate the development of a proposed remedies package that comprehensively addresses the concerns of multiple authorities.[170] In some circumstances, cooperation may result in one authority closing an investigation without remedies after taking another authority's remedies into account.[171]

Illustrative Example H

Situation: After investigating the merger as outlined in Illustrative Example G, the U.S. Agency finds that the merger is likely to substantially lessen competition in the U.S. market for Product X, and therefore that the merger would violate Section 7 of the Clayton Act. The U.S. Agency determines that these competitive concerns likely can be addressed through a divestiture of Corporation 1's assets related to Product X. Countries Alpha, Beta, and Gamma also find that the merger will harm competition in their markets for Product X, and Country Gamma has additional concerns about a reduction of competition in Gamma's market for Product Y.

Discussion: The U.S. Agency and the authorities in Alpha, Beta, and Gamma discuss, among themselves and with Corporation 1 and Corporation 2, a proposed remedy for the competitive concerns regarding Product X, in an effort to identify a package of assets for divesture that addresses the reviewing agencies' competitive concerns.

---

[169] As with other aspects of cooperation, a person's grant of waivers can enhance the efficacy of such discussions between the Agencies and foreign authorities.

[170] *See* U.S.- Can. Working Grp., *Best Practices on Cooperation in Merger Investigations* (2014), https://www.ftc.gov/system/files/attachments/international-competition-consumer-protection-cooperation-agreements/canada-us_merger_cooperation_best_practices.pdf; US-EU Merger Working Grp., *Best Practices on Cooperation in Merger Investigations* (2011), https://www.justice.gov/sites/default/files/atr/legacy/2011/10/27/276276.pdf.

[171] *See* United States Submission to OECD Competition Committee regarding Remedies in Cross-Border Merger Cases, DAF/COMP/WP3/WD(2013) (discussing cooperation and remedies in: *In the Matter of Agilent Technologies*; *In the Matter of Panasonic Corporation/Sanyo Electric Co., Ltd.*; *UTC/Goodrich; Cisco/Tandberg;* and other matters).

In this instance, the U.S. Agency and the foreign reviewing authorities agree that the same divestiture remedy for Product X will effectively address the competitive concerns in their respective jurisdictions. Corporation 1 and Corporation 2 enter into a consent decree in the United States that includes divestiture of specified assets of Corporation 1's related to Product X, and the authority in Alpha seeks the same divestiture remedy to ensure enforceability of the remedy in its jurisdiction. Country Beta concludes that the remedies secured in the United States and in Country Alpha are sufficient to address its competitive concerns and closes its investigation. Country Gamma seeks a remedy identical to that entered into in the United States and Country Alpha regarding Product X, coupled with an additional remedy to address the competitive harm in its jurisdiction regarding Product Y.

5.2 Special Considerations in Criminal Investigations

Among the Department's top priorities is the criminal investigation and prosecution of international price-fixing cartels. Because these cartels often involve foreign-located defendants, witnesses, and evidence, antitrust enforcement in this context can present not only an investigatory challenge but also a special need for international cooperation and coordination. Mutual Legal Assistance Treaties ("MLATs") are an important basis for international cooperation in the Department's criminal antitrust enforcement. MLATs are used often in criminal investigations to gather evidence located outside the United States. Parties to these agreements have agreed to assist one another in criminal law enforcement matters.[172] The specific provisions of MLATs vary, but they generally provide for assistance in obtaining evidence and in serving documents in one jurisdiction at the request of the other.

The Department also coordinates with foreign authorities when they are conducting cartel investigations parallel with the Department's own. The Department sometimes shares information to coordinate investigative steps. For example, to minimize the risk of document destruction, the Department and foreign authorities can time dawn raids and searches to coincide in multiple jurisdictions. And the

---

[172] The United States' MLAT with Germany is unique in that it also provides for U.S. assistance to Germany in administrative cartel matters. *See* Mutual Legal Assistance Treaty, U.S.-Ger., S. Treaty Doc. 108-27 (2003), *available at* https://www.congress.gov/108/cdoc/tdoc27/CDOC-108tdoc27.pdf.

Department and foreign authorities may also coordinate on logistical aspects of their parallel investigations to help minimize overlapping and inconsistent demands placed on cooperating individuals and firms. The Department recognizes that such coordination has the benefit of decreasing the costs to cooperators and increasing the pace of the investigations and is committed to engaging in such coordination where practicable.

The Department's ability to share information with foreign authorities is not unlimited, however. An essential component in the investigation and enforcement of the criminal antitrust laws is the grand jury, which is subject to the grand jury secrecy rule. Through its subpoenas, a grand jury can "compel the production of evidence or the testimony of witnesses as it considers appropriate, and its operation generally is unrestrained by the technical procedural and evidentiary rules governing the conduct of criminal trials."[173] The Department is prohibited, however, from disclosing matters occurring before the grand jury absent an applicable exception.[174] This prohibition cannot be waived by a subject of the investigation, a grand jury witness, or a recipient of a grand jury subpoena. The prohibition, however, does not apply to these persons and therefore does not generally prohibit disclosures by them.

In addition, a criminal investigation can gather information through the assistance of an applicant under the Department's Corporate and Individual Leniency Policies for antitrust crimes.[175] To qualify for leniency under those policies, the applicant is required, among other things, to report the wrongdoing with candor and completeness and provide full, continuing, and complete cooperation. That required cooperation includes the production of all documents, information, or other materials in the applicant's possession, custody, or control, wherever located, that are requested by the Department in connection with the criminal antitrust investigation and are not protected by the attorney-client privilege or the work-product doctrine.

---

[173] *United States v. Calandra*, 414 U.S. 338, 343 (1974); *see also Branzburg v. Hayes*, 408 U.S. 665, 688 (1972). The "powers of the grand jury are not unlimited," *id.*; for example, a grand jury subpoena does not override a valid privilege and may be quashed or modified by a court if compliance would be "unreasonable or oppressive." Fed. R. Crim. P. 17(c)(2).

[174] Fed. R. Crim. P. 6(e).

[175] For information on these policies, see https://www.justice.gov/atr/leniency-program.

The Department holds the identity of leniency applicants and the information they provide in strict confidence. The Department does not publicly disclose the identity of an applicant or information provided by the applicant, absent prior disclosure by the applicant, unless required to do so by a court order in connection with litigation. A leniency applicant can agree to waive this confidentiality assurance and allow the Department to share the applicant's identity and information with a foreign authority. Such waivers of confidentiality for information sharing with a foreign authority are common when the applicant has also applied for leniency under the foreign authority's leniency policy.

Lastly, the Department sometimes seeks the cooperation of foreign jurisdictions to obtain indicted fugitives. It can seek the issuance of an INTERPOL "Red Notice," which operates as an international "wanted" notice that, in some INTERPOL member countries, serves as a request, should the fugitive enter their jurisdiction, to arrest the subject, with a view toward extradition. And the Department can request that a foreign jurisdiction extradite a fugitive defendant located in that jurisdiction to the United States.[176]

---

[176] Extradition ordinarily depends on the presence and terms of an extradition treaty with the foreign jurisdiction.

Annex 1. Defined Terms

ACPERA............................	Antitrust Criminal Penalty Enhancement and Reform Act of 2004
Agencies...........................	The Department of Justice and Federal Trade Commission
APEC...............................	Asia-Pacific Economic Cooperation
CID.................................	Civil Investigative Demand
Clayton Act.......................	Clayton Antitrust Act
Commission.......................	Federal Trade Commission
Department.......................	The Department of Justice
ETC Act...........................	Export Trading Company Act of 1982
ETCR..............................	Export Trade Certificate of Review
FTC................................	Federal Trade Commission
FTC Act...........................	Federal Trade Commission Act
FSIA...............................	Foreign Sovereign Immunities Act of 1976
FTAIA.............................	Foreign Trade Antitrust Improvements Act of 1982
FOIA...............................	Freedom of Information Act
HSR Act...........................	Hart-Scott-Rodino Antitrust Improvements Act of 1976
HSR Rules........................	Hart-Scott-Rodino Premerger Notification Rules
IAEAA.............................	International Antitrust Enforcement Assistance Act
ICN................................	International Competition Network
International Guidelines........................	Antitrust Guidelines for International Enforcement and Cooperation
MLATs.............................	Mutual Legal Assistance Treaties
NCRPA............................	National Cooperative Research and Production Act
OECD..............................	Organisation for Economic Co-operation and Development
Sherman Act......................	Sherman Antitrust Act
SDOs..............................	Standards Development Organizations
UNCTAD..........................	United Nations Conference on Trade and Development
USTR..............................	U.S. Trade Representative

www.ingramcontent.com/pod-product-compliance
Lightning Source LLC
Chambersburg PA
CBHW081259180526
45170CB00007B/2487

* 9 7 8 1 5 4 2 5 7 5 6 4 5 *